Survey of the Scriptures
BASIC BIBLE COMMENTARY

Matthew

Gospel of the King

Dr. J. Arthur Springer

MERIDIAN

Copyright © 1991 by Meridian

This edition is published by special arrangement with and permission of Moody External Studies. Revised edition by Moody External Studies of the USA.

First edition © 1954 by Moody Bible Institute of the USA.

All rights reserved.

No part of this book may be reproduced in any form without written permission from Moody Bible Institute, 820 N. La Salle Dr., Chicago, IL 60610.

Note: Archaic expressions, spellings, and punctuation have been updated in some Bible verses.

M19 Paperback Study Edition
ISBN: 0-529-06949-0

Cover design by Gayle Raymer
Book Design by Blue Water Ink

A Meridian Publication
Published with World Bible Publishers

Printed in the United States of America

Contents

	Preface	5
	Introduction	7
1	An Overview	9
2	The King Is Born (1–2)	19
3	The King Is Introduced (3–4)	25
4	The King Declares the Principles of the Kingdom (5–7)	35
5	The King Presents His Credentials (8–10)	49
6	The King Declares His Rejection (11–12)	59
7	The King Declares the Mysteries of the Kingdom (13)	69

8	The King Presents Additional Credentials (14–15)	77
9	The King Promises to Build His Church (16–18)	85
10	The King Enters Jerusalem (19–21)	99
11	The King Teaches and Reproves (22–23)	113
12	The King Foretells the Coming Kingdom (24–25)	123
13	The King Is Betrayed, Condemned, and Denied (26)	133
14	The King Dies and Rises Again (27–28)	143

Preface

To begin to understand the specifics of in-depth Bible study, we must have a grasp of how the entire Bible fits together and the basic theme of each Bible book.

Survey of the Scriptures first takes us on an exciting tour through the Bible, relating one section to another. So that by knowing how each part relates to the others we can better appreciate and apply its lessons for us.

J. Arthur Springer was at Moody Bible Institute from 1944 to 1967 where he developed and taught this basic Bible study guide. For over thirty-five years it has been part of a Bible correspondence course for the External Studies division of Moody Bible Institute.

Now for the first time, this incisive and insightful study is available for personal or group Bible study to help readers see the Scriptures as an interrelated unit with a plan, a plot, and a purpose and to provide a more in-depth look at each individual book of the Bible.

—The Publisher

Introduction

To see the Bible as a whole is not only vital to a proper understanding of the Bible; it can also be a thrilling experience!

This book and others in the Survey of the Scripture series provide study material on individual books of the Bible for a closer look at specific areas of Scripture.

The Gospel of Matthew occupies a strategic place among the four Gospels as the connecting link between the Old Testament and the New. The long-promised Messiah of Israel is introduced in the opening verse as "Jesus Christ, the son of David, the son of Abraham."

To understand this Gospel correctly is to put Israel in her proper place in the plan of God. This Mr. Springer has done in a thorough, sane, sound, scriptural way in *Matthew: The Gospel of the King*.

This commentary, rather than being a complete study of the book of Matthew, furnishes an introduction to start you on a lifetime of Bible study and Christian growth.

Because these materials were initially used both as classroom and correspondence school texts, the style is one of a teacher—guiding, challenging, directing, stimulating, and raising questions as well as providing answers.

The author, J. Arthur Springer, was Professor of Bible for over twenty-three years at Moody Bible Institute. In this study he explains the background and content of the Gospel of Matthew, emphasizes the royal image of Jesus, and explores the kingdom of God that Christ came to establish.

The content of this edition is taken from an adult credit course from Moody Bible Institute, External Studies Division. For information on how you might take this and other courses for credit, write for a free catalog to:

Moody External Studies
Moody Bible Institute
820 N. La Salle
Chicago, IL 60610

1

An Overview

THE PURPOSE OF OUR STUDY

1. Why four Gospels?

Across the centuries that have intervened since "the days of his flesh," four accounts, and only four, have come down to us concerning the incarnation and earthly life of the Son of God. These four accounts—each one the product of the man whose name it bears—stand in order at the beginning of the New Testament.

a. The four evangelists

Matthew and John were written by men who were numbered among his twelve apostles and who thus were eyewitnesses of most of the events they record. The other two, Mark and Luke, while written by men not numbered among the Twelve, were nevertheless produced by men who knew the facts from close association with those who were eyewitnesses.

b. A fourfold portrait of Christ

None of these accounts is a biography of the Lord. Rather, each one gives us certain facts concerning his life, as seen from a certain vantage point. Matthew presents to us the *King*; Mark shows us the *Servant*; Luke, the *Son of Man*; and John, the *Son of God*.

This does not mean that Mark, Luke, and John have nothing to say about his being King; or that Matthew, Mark, and Luke say nothing about his being the Son of God. On the other hand, the distinctive points of view that characterize the various Gospels are those mentioned.

To understand fully his purpose in coming to earth, we must stand beside Matthew and with him cry out in the words of Zechariah (9:9), "Behold your King!" Then we must look at him as Mark does, and with him say, "Amen," to the words of God spoken through Isaiah, "Behold my servant!" (42:1). Again, we must take our place with Luke and with him exclaim as does Zechariah in another place, "Behold the man!" (6:12). Finally we need to take John's point of view, and with him cry in wonder and faith in the words of Isaiah, "Behold your God!" (40:9).

2. Matthew—the book of the kingdom of heaven

Many and varied are the theories abroad today regarding the kingdom of God and the kingdom of heaven. Some maintain, for instance, that these two kingdoms are identical; others, that they are distinct. Some say the "kingdom" is here in the world today and is identical with Christianity. They do not differentiate between the two expressions. Others assert that the kingdom will not be on earth in any vital sense until the return of our Lord

Jesus Christ. Many other theories are advanced, as well as variations of those mentioned above.

SOURCE AND BACKGROUND OF THE KINGDOM IDEA

Both the concept of God as King and that of a kingdom on earth over which he should rule occur early in the Word of God. However, other kings and kingdoms are mentioned first—the natural preceding the spiritual. This is in keeping with the principle embodied in 1 Corinthians 15:46: "That was not first which is spiritual, but that which is natural; and afterward that which is spiritual."

1. The first use of *kingdom* and *king* in the Bible

In Genesis 10:10, the word *kingdom* occurs for the first time. There Nimrod's kingdom is referred to as starting with Babel. In the next chapter the Tower of Babel was the cause of the division of the race into various nations and languages. Then in Genesis 14:1, the word *king* occurs for the first time. Here we meet nine kings and their kingdoms—four of them pitted against the other five in warfare.

2. Israel's demand for a king

In 1 Samuel 8 the people of Israel demand a king like those of the nations around them; they had rejected God's direct rule over them.

3. Early references to the kingdom of the Lord

In Chronicles there are four references, at least, to the kingdom of the Lord. 1 Chronicles 28:5 refers to Solomon as being chosen "to sit upon the throne of the kingdom of the Lord over Israel." In 1 Chronicles 29:11, David says, Yours is the kingdom, O LORD"; in verse 23, the sacred historian says, "Solomon sat on the throne of the LORD as king"; and in 2 Chronicles 13:8, Abijah speaks of "the kingdom of the LORD in the hand of the sons of David." These four all refer to an earthly kingdom ruled over by purely human kings, although on behalf of the Lord, whose kingdom it is recognized to be.

4. Prophecies of Christ's kingdom

When we turn to the Psalms, the expectation of an earthly kingdom, over which the Lord himself will one day reign, is very clear indeed. In Psalm 2, God says prophetically concerning his Son, "Yet have I set my king upon my holy hill of Zion"; and in Psalm 45, "Your throne, O God, is for ever and ever: the scepter of your kingdom is a right scepter."

As we go on through the prophetic books of the Old Testament and human failure becomes more evident, these predictions become more and more pronounced until we come to the New Testament. In the Gospel of Matthew, which opens the New Testament, we have a thorough unfolding of the idea of a kingdom over which Christ is to reign personally—the kingdom of heaven. This idea is developed in other parts of the New Testament; and in Revelation the Lord Jesus Christ is seen coming back to assume the reins of government on earth.

THE PHRASE "KINGDOM OF HEAVEN"

The precise phrase "kingdom of heaven" occurs thirty-three times in Matthew and nowhere else in the Bible.

The idea appears in Daniel 2:44 and elsewhere but not the exact phrase. See, for example, Isaiah 9:7; Daniel 7:14, 27; and Obadiah 21.

THE AUTHORSHIP OF THIS GOSPEL

According to abundant tradition, Matthew was written by that member of the Twelve whose name it bears, perhaps within ten or fifteen years after the Lord's resurrection, thus before A.D. 45. The author was Matthew, the publican, called Levi by Mark and Luke (cf. Matthew 9:9; 10:3; Mark 2:14; Luke 5:27). Some have argued that Matthew was written after Mark; but the unanimous voice of ancient tradition puts Matthew first.

THE PERSONS ADDRESSED

Matthew addresses his Gospel to his fellow countrymen, the Jews. There are many proofs of this:
 1. Christ's genealogy is traced from Abraham, the father of all the Jews, through David, their most illustrious king.
 2. There are many references to and quotations from the Old Testament, with which ordinarily only Jews would at that time be familiar.
 3. The Sermon on the Mount, which is based squarely on the Mosaic Law, is given the most extended report found in any of the Gospels.
 4. Emphasis is laid throughout on the kingdom of heaven, which pertains basically to Israel.

THE THEME OF THIS GOSPEL

The theme is *the King and the kingdom.* The four Gospels present the same glorious Person but in varying aspects. In the first Gospel he is the King; in the second, the Servant—the faithful Servant of Jehovah—come to do the will of God; in the third, the Son of Man—the representative Man, living for God's glory and dying for man's sin; and the fourth, the Son of God, the Word made flesh.

Yet each Gospel has some of all the pictures of Christ. His kingship and his deity, for instance, are set forth in Luke 1:32–35; whereas his service to his Father is emphasized in Luke 2:49. His humanity and service are both stressed in Matthew 20:28 and his deity in Matthew 16:16–17.

In Matthew he is preeminently the King, and this aspect and the fact of the kingdom is constantly under consideration.

THE MATERIAL IN THIS GOSPEL

The character of the material in the book of Matthew is fourfold. That is, the great bulk of the contents of the book may be divided into four classifications: *incidents, miracles, teaching, and prophecy.* Of each of these four classes of material, there is much in the first Gospel. Incident follows incident and miracle follows miracle in quick succession, although the greatest concentrations of miracles are found in chapters 8–10 and in chapters 14–15. There is teaching in Matthew 5–7 and 13; while chapters 24 and 25 are wholly given over to teaching. Prophecy also holds a prominent place in this Gospel. Prophetic material is scattered throughout the book, and in chapters 24 and 25 the teaching is entirely of this character.

THE HISTORY IN THIS GOSPEL

The main historical elements of the book of Matthew may be classified under six heads: *the birth of Christ, his life, his miracles, his teaching, his death, and his resurrection.*

THE ASPECTS OF THE KINGDOM

While the theme of Matthew is the kingdom of heaven, the aspects in which the Kingdom is presented vary within the book itself. These may be divided in a threefold way:

1. **Chapters 1—12**

    The kingdom of heaven is offered to the Jews and rejected by them.

2. **Chapter 13**

    The mysteries of the kingdom of heaven are presented, that aspect in which the kingdom exists in this dispensation of grace.

3. **Chapters 24 and 25**

    In the Olivet Discourse, the kingdom is presented prophetically, as it will one day be established on earth by our Lord Jesus Christ at his Second Coming.

A PREVIEW OF THIS GOSPEL

The main points of the Gospel in its description of the King are as follows:

1. Son of David and therefore heir to David's throne and kingdom on the basis of 2 Samuel 7:12–13 (chapter 1, especially vv. 1, 6, 16).

2. Son of Abraham and therefore the channel through whom God's blessing should flow to all nations, as promised in Genesis 22:18 (chapter 1, especially vv. 1–2, 16).

3. King of the Jews from his birth (chapter 2, especially v. 2).

4. The King's statement of the principles of the kingdom (chapters 5—7; especially 5:3, 10, 19, 20; 6:10, 33; 7:21).

5. The King's preaching the Gospel of the kingdom (9:35; cf. 4:17, 23; 10:7).

6. The King's virtual rejection (chapters 11–12; especially 11:12, 16–19; 12:24).

7. The King's teaching concerning the mysteries of the kingdom (chapter 13, especially vv. 11, 24, 31, 33, 44, 45, 47).

8. The King's prophecy of the church (16:18; cf. 18:17).

9. The King's transfiguration in his kingdom glory (chapter 17, especially vv. 1–2).

10. The King's commendation of self-sacrifice for the sake of the kingdom (19:21).

11. The King's statement of a prime characteristic of citizens of the kingdom: humility (19:14).

12. The King's statement concerning the difficulty of a rich man to enter the kingdom (19:23).

13. The King's prophecy concerning the position of the Twelve in the future kingdom (19:28).

14. The King's teaching concerning his sovereignty (20:1–16, especially v. 15).

15. The King's exhortation to humility in connection with the kingdom (20:20–28, especially vv. 26–28).

16. The King's official entrance into Jerusalem (21:1–17, especially vv. 5, 9).

17. The King's prophecy of the Jews' forfeiture of the kingdom to another nation (21:18–46, especially v. 43).

18. The King's prediction concerning the future Kingdom (chapters 24;25; especially 25:1, 34, 40).

19. The King's rejection and crucifixion (chapters 26–27, especially 26:63–66; 27:22, 29, 35, 37).

20. The King's resurrection; his authority; his commission to his disciples (chapter 28, especially vv. 6, 18–20).

2

The King Is Born

1:1–2:23

THE GENEALOGY OF THE KING (1:1–17)

1. **"Jesus Christ, the son of David, the son of Abraham" (1:1)**

The book of Matthew first presents Jesus Christ as a descendant of David and of Abraham. This means that he was not merely of the seed of Abraham according to the flesh but also of the house of David and thus of the royal family of Israel. As "seed of Abraham," he would be eligible to fulfill God's promise to Abraham, that in his seed all the nations of the earth were to be blessed. (See Genesis 22:18.) As Son of David, he would be eligible to sit on David's throne, the throne of Israel. (See 2 Samuel

7:13, 16; Psalm 89:35–37; Jeremiah 33:15–17. Observe how these Old Testament prophecies guarantee an eternal throne on which a descendant of David was to sit.)

2. The genealogies of Matthew and Luke compared

There are several differences between the genealogies in Matthew 1 and Luke 3. First, Matthew starts in antiquity and traces the line down to Christ; whereas Luke starts with Christ and goes back. Second, Matthew seems to be interested in the Lord's genealogy merely from Abraham down, while Luke goes back past Abraham to Adam and even to God. Third, the names in the two genealogies are almost entirely different between David and the Lord Jesus. Matthew's list contains the names of most of the kings of Judah; whereas Luke's list has none but that of David.

Matthew 1:16 and Luke 3:23 explain the lists. In Matthew "Jacob begat Joseph," proving that Joseph was the natural son of Jacob. In Luke there is no word for "son" in the Greek text. Joseph was "of Heli," which probably means that Joseph was the son-in-law of Heli. That is to say, Matthew gives Joseph's line; whereas Luke provides Mary's line. Matthew traces Jesus' genealogy through the line of kings and to Joseph, his foster father and legal father. Luke tracks his genealogy through Mary, his natural but virgin mother.

3. The forms of proper names

In the genealogy in Matthew 1, the Greek forms of the names are given in the King James Version; whereas in the New American Standard Bible the familiar Hebrew forms are used. Look at verses 6–11 in the New American

Standard Bible (NASB) and count the names of the kings of Judah given there.

4. The virgin birth of Christ declared

Note how carefully Matthew's statement is made in 1:16 concerning the birth of Jesus. He was born of Mary but not begotten of Joseph. This vital point is made again and again in the next division.

THE BIRTH OF THE KING (1:18–25)

1. Further proof of the virgin birth (vv. 18–20, 24, 25)

These verses describe the manner of the King's advent. He might have entered the world as a full-grown man, but comes as a baby. Not only so, but repeatedly it is stated, in various ways, that he is virgin-born. We see it in verse 18, in the statement "before they came together." Joseph was not the father; "she was found with child of the Holy Spirit," which indicates that it was the power of God working in her to produce the miracle of the virgin birth.

Joseph was under the impression at first that Mary was an impure woman and planned to reject her privately, probably in accordance with Deuteronomy 24:1. But an angel appeared to him and informed him of the facts of the case (v. 20).

Once more, in verses 24–25, the fact of the virgin birth is stated, making at least five times where that truth is directly affirmed or implied in the last ten verses of chapter 1.

2. "Jesus . . . Emmanuel" (vv. 21-23)

Note the name to be given the child and the reason for the name "Jesus," which means "Savior"; for the angel says, "He shall save his people from their sins." Note also that the prophecy of Isaiah 7:14 is applied to Jesus and the meaning of the prophetic name "Emmanuel," "God with us." The meaning tells about his person, who he is, and about his work, what he is to do.

THE WORSHIP OF THE KING (2:1-12)

Bethlehem—Herod—the Magi—the star

Chapter 2 begins with the birthplace of Jesus and gives the name of the reigning king in Judea at that time. Bethlehem was about five miles from Jerusalem, almost due south. Herod was not of the line of David; he was not even an Israelite but an Idumean, of the land formerly known as Edom.

Wise men—that is, Magi, or learned men, such as those referred to in Esther 1:13 and Daniel 2:12—came from the East to Jerusalem at about that time. They came seeking one born King of the Jews. Note the unusual expression "born King," not "born to be King." Evidently they have sufficient spiritual discernment to realize that the one they seek was King at his birth and not merely one who was to grow up to be King. Their purpose is to worship him. Herod is disturbed when he hears about the one "born King of the Jews." If true, this is a direct threat to his throne, or at least to the succession of his son or sons to that throne. To his question as to where Christ, or the Messiah of Old Testament prophecy, was to be born, the chief priests and scribes reply, "In Bethlehem of

Judea." This they know, as we learn in verses 5–6, from Micah 5:2, which should be compared with Matthew 2:6. Herod, pretending that he too desires to worship the new-born Christ, sends the wise men to Bethlehem with instructions to let him know when they have found him.

The wise men had seen his star in the East and now the star reappears and leads them to the house in which the young child is sheltered with his mother, Mary. That this was not a heavenly body—an ordinary star, comet, or planet—seems rather certain, as no such distant body can possibly indicate a particular object on earth such as a house. It seems likely, therefore, that this was something close to the earth, provided by the Lord to guide the wise men—something that probably they alone could see. When they see the infant Jesus, they worship him and give him gifts.

We do not know how many wise men there were, although tradition says three. In any case, they brought three kinds of gifts: gold, frankincense, and myrrh. The costly gold was probably in acknowledgement of his deity; the frankincense, in token of his humanity; and the bitter myrrh, in recognition of the purpose of his incarnation, namely, death in order to "save his people from their sins" (1:21). Having finished their mission, they return to their own country by a different route, God having warned them not to go back to Herod.

THE INFANCY OF THE KING (2:13-23)

1. The flight into Egypt (vv. 13-15)

The latter part of chapter 2 tells of Herod's wicked but fruitless attempt to kill the infant Jesus. An angel appears to Joseph and warns him to take Jesus and Mary and flee to Egypt to escape the murderous intentions of Herod. Joseph obeys, remaining in Egypt until Herod's death, which takes place shortly. In verse 15 there is a quotation from Hosea 11:1. The prophet refers directly to Israel, the nation God had called out of Egypt in the time of Moses to lead them to Canaan. Matthew applies the reference to Christ in connection with the fact that God called him out of Egypt to return to the same Promised Land to fulfill the functions of the Messiah.

2. The slaughter of the innocents (vv. 16–18)

When Herod realizes that the wise men are not going to return to tell him where the child is who was "born King of the Jews," he decides to have all the male children (NASB) in Bethlehem killed, from the age of two years down. But he is too late; the infant Jesus has already been taken to Egypt.

3. The return to Nazareth (vv. 19–23)

After the death of Herod, an angel appears again to Joseph and instructs him to return to the land of Israel with Jesus and Mary. This he does, but he avoids Judea where Herod's son Archelaus is now king. He goes north into Galilee to the city of Nazareth, of which city he and Mary are both citizens.

3

The King Is Introduced

3:1–4:25

THE HERALD OF THE KING (3:1-12)

1. John the Baptist

In Matthew 3 John the Baptist is presented for the first time as a grown man.

The first twelve verses tell at least six things about the man. His *parish* was the wilderness of Judea, a most unlikely place, humanly speaking, for a preaching ministry (v. 1). His *preaching*, however, was characterized by such tremendous power that "Jerusalem, and all Judea, and all the region round about Jordan" went out into the wilderness to hear him and were profoundly affected by his preaching (vv. 5-6). His *message* was one of repentance and confession of sin (vv. 2, 6). His *clothing* was rough and simple—a garment of camel's hair gathered about his waist with a girdle or belt of leather (v. 4). His *diet*, too, was exceedingly simple—locusts and wild honey (v. 4). His *baptism* was "with water unto repentance" (v. 11).

2. The message of John

Note how his message is summarized in verse 2: "Repent ... for the kingdom of heaven is at hand."

This brief message consists of two parts, an exhortation and a reason. The exhortation is simply "Repent." The reason is that "the kingdom of heaven is at hand." That is to say, the kingdom promised in the Old Testament is about to be offered to Israel. However, there is one condition to the immediate establishment of the kingdom and that is repentance on the part of the people.

The message is amplified in verses 7–12 where John addresses himself to certain of the Pharisees and Sadducees who appear in the crowd. To them he speaks words of reproof, warning, and exhortation.

By way of reproof he calls them a "generation of vipers."

In warning he speaks of several things: "the wrath to come" (v. 7), the folly of depending on the mere fact that they are descendants of Abraham (v. 9), and the imminence of the day of reckoning for the Jews (v. 10).

By way of exhortation he urges them to bring forth fruits for repentance (v. 8). He did not tell them God would not save them until they produce the fruits of good works but rather that he himself will not baptize them until they display the evidence that their repentance is genuine.

3. The baptism of John

With respect to his baptism, the following facts should be noted: First, it is not Christian baptism but a baptism "unto repentance" (v. 11). Both are symbolic, but they symbolize different truths. Christian baptism symbolizes our transference from the realm of the world, the flesh, and the devil to the realm of the Father, the Son, and the Holy Spirit; and it indicates that the person receiving it has trusted Christ as Savior and has been forgiven by the Father and baptized with the Holy Spirit. John's baptism, however, symbolized that the person baptized had genuinely repented and was looking forward to the kingdom.

Second, John contrasts his baptism with that bestowed by the King. To begin with, the King is incomparably greater than John (v. 11), which indicates that the King's baptism is incomparably more important than John's. Then, too, John's baptism is "with water," whereas the King's is "with the Holy Spirit, and with fire" (v. 11). In other words, John's baptism is symbolic, while the King's is real—either with the Holy Spirit, in answer to faith; or with fire, in judgment for unbelief.

Finally, John's baptism is "unto repentance," whereas the King's is unto a separation of wheat from chaff. The wheat is fruit for God; the chaff is worthless, something to be burned up (v. 12).

THE BAPTISM OF THE KING (3:13–17)

1. John's protest (3:14)

While John baptizes in the Jordan River, Jesus—now grown to manhood—comes from Galilee to be baptized by him (v. 13). John, however, protests on the ground that it would be more fitting for him to be baptized by Jesus (v. 14). This is not to be understood as meaning that John knew at this time that Jesus was the Messiah, the Son of God. He did not know this until after he had baptized Jesus, as we are told in John 1:31–34.

The descent of the Holy Spirit in the form of a dove, which takes place at the conclusion of Jesus' baptism, was the prearranged sign from heaven whereby John was to know that Jesus was the Son of God. His protest then was apparently based on the fact that John knew Jesus possessed character and godliness superior to his own.

2. The Lord Jesus' answer (3:15)

Jesus answers John's protest and says, "Thus it becomes us to fulfill all righteousness." By this he probably means that he wants to undergo John's baptism to accomplish the following:

a. *Put his stamp of approval on John, his message, and his baptism.*

b. *Become temporarily—until he should be declared publicly to be the Messiah—a disciple of John.*

c. *Start that long process of identifying himself with his people's sin,* which was prophesied in Matthew 1:21, and which was to find its culmination at the cross where he was made to be sin for us in order "that we might be made the righteousness of God in him." See 2 Corinthians 5:21.

3. The Father speaking; the Holy Spirit descending; the Son receiving baptism (vv. 16–17)

After John baptizes him, Jesus goes up out of the waters of the Jordan. As he does a remarkable thing occurs.

Matthew says the heavens were opened to *him*, and that *he* "saw the Spirit of God descending like a dove, and lighting upon him." John the Baptist said in John 1:32–34 that he *saw* this, and by it knew the Lord's indentity. As a result, he testified that he was the Son of God. Furthermore, Matthew says a voice from heaven said: "This is my beloved Son, in whom I am well pleased" (v. 17). Mark recorded that the voice from heaven said: "You are my beloved Son . . ." (1:11). Accordingly, the Father declares the double fact—that Jesus was his Son and that he was perfectly satisfied with him—both to Jesus himself ("You are"), and to John and other bystanders ("This is").

At Jesus' baptism the three Persons in the Godhead are specifically brought together for the first time in Scripture. The Father speaks from heaven; the Holy Spirit descends; and the Son receives baptism, which was the Holy Spirit's enduement for his public ministry and the Father's testimony to Jesus' person and conduct.

THE TEMPTATION OF THE KING (4:1–11)

1. The temptation: proof of Jesus' sinlessness

Matthew 4:1 says Jesus was led by the Spirit into the wilderness to be tempted by the devil. Temptation is a complex matter. God has his gracious hand in it, and Satan has his vicious hand in it as well. This was true also in the case of Job. It is true here. God's purpose is to demonstrate that his beloved Son could not yield to temptation. Satan's purpose is just the opposite, to persuade the Son of God, if possible, to abandon his absolute dependence on his Father and thus commit sin.

2. A threefold temptation

The temptation of our Lord is divided into three phases, much as was the temptation of Eve, in Genesis 3. The three phases in each case correspond to the three parts of our human being: body, soul, and spirit. In Genesis 3:6 we read that "the woman saw that the tree was good for food [the body], and that it was pleasant to the eyes [the soul], and a tree to be desired to make one wise," [the spirit]. In Matthew 4 the devil tempts the Lord Jesus similarly. The suggestion to make the stones into bread has to do with the body. The temptation to cast himself down from the eminence of the Temple, to be received and acclaimed by the people below as they see him glide down to them, has to do with the soul and its ambitions. The suggestion to fall down and worship Satan and so receive the worship of the kingdoms of the world, has to do with the spirit, in which realm worship is offered either to God or to another.

3. The threefold "It is written"

Satan comes to Jesus after he has fasted forty days, apparently assuming he will have more chance of overcoming the Lord's resistance to temptation when his physical strength is at low ebb. In each instance the Lord meets the temptation with the Word of God. Each time he quotes from the book of Deuteronomy, saying, "It is written."

4. Jesus' complete obedience to his Father

The Lord put his Father first in each phase of the triple temptation. In the *first*, when Satan says, "If you are the Son of God, command that these stones be made bread" (v. 3), Jesus replies by quoting Deuteronomy 8:3. "Man shall not live by bread alone, but by every word that proceeds out of the mouth of God." Whatever else this may signify, it means that, even though he was the Son of God and thus possessed the power to perform the suggested miracle, he would not do it because he had no authority to do so.

In the *second* phase of the temptation, the devil suggests to him: "If you are the Son of God, cast yourself down." To support this suggestion, he misquotes Psalm 91. Compare the quotation in Matthew 4:6 with the original in Psalm 91:11–12 and observe what Satan omitted. Again the Lord Jesus answers him from a Scripture that puts God first. "You shall not tempt the Lord your God," he quotes from Deuteronomy 6:16.

Once more, in the *third* and last phase of the temptation, Satan shows Christ all the kingdoms of the world, and says, "All these things will I give you, if you will fall down and worship me" (v. 9). To this blasphemous suggestion Jesus responds with a third quotation from Scripture, putting the Father first again. "You shall worship the Lord your God, and him only shall you serve" (Deuteronomy 6:13–14). Then he dismisses the devil with these words, "Get out of here, Satan!" With the temptation concluded, Satan leaves and angels minister to the Lord Jesus.

THE EARLY GALILEAN MINISTRY OF THE KING (4:12–25)

1. From Nazareth to Capernaum; the Lord's message of repentance (vv. 12–17)

After this John the Baptist is cast into prison. Jesus, hearing this, goes into Galilee. He moves from Nazareth, where he was brought up, to another Galilean city, Capernaum, on the edge of the Sea of Galilee, about twenty miles to the northeast. The reason for transferring his home from Nazareth to Capernaum is suggested in Luke 4 as being his rejection in the former city.

Matthew says that our Lord's move to Capernaum fulfilled the prophecy of Isaiah 9:1-2 concerning a great light springing up in Galilee in the territory of Zebulun and Naphtali (vv. 13-16). Matthew reports that from that time on Jesus began to preach, saying, "Repent: for the kingdom of heaven is at hand" (v. 17).

This is precisely the message preached by John the Baptist (Matthew 3:2). Thus we learn that Jesus, at the beginning of his public ministry, offered the kingdom to the people on the condition of their repentance, just as John the Baptist, his herald, had done.

2. The call of four of the Twelve (vv. 18-22)

First, Jesus calls two fishermen brothers from their fishing. He challenges Simon Peter and Andrew, "Follow me, and I will make you fishers of men" (v. 19). They are accustomed to catching natural fish, either for themselves or for the market. Jesus promises to make them fishers of men—proficient at catching human beings for Christ and for heaven. But note the condition: "Follow me!" They hear the call, accept the challenge, and make the sacrifice. They do it at once (v. 20).

A little farther on he sees another pair of brothers, also fishermen—James and John, the sons of Zebedee (v. 21). He calls them, too, and they also follow him immediately (v. 22). These two have to leave the ship and their father, with whom apparently they have been in partnership.

3. The early days of our Lord's public ministry in Galilee (vv. 23-25)

Matthew writes that in these early days of Jesus' ministry he does three things (v. 23). First, he travels throughout Galilee; second, as he does so, he teaches and preaches in the Jewish synagogues all through that section of the country; and third, he heals the people of all sorts of sickness and disease. His fame travels throughout the whole of the Roman province of Syria, which includes a large amount of territory to the northeast of Galilee—so much so that persons afflicted with diseases of various kinds, demon-possessed people, epileptics, and paralytics, are brought to him and he heals them (v. 24 NASB). Not only so but great multitudes follow him from Galilee, his home country; from Decapolis, a section of country southeast of Galilee; from Jerusalem and Judea, to the south; and from the territory beyond Jordan, which included Perea (v. 25).

Thus, we observe several things with reference to these early days of our Lord's public ministry in Galilee. First, *his message* (vv. 17, 23); second, *the extent of his travels* (v. 23); third, *his fame* (v. 24); fourth, *his healing power* (vv. 23-24); and fifth, *his popularity* (v. 25).

4

The King Declares the Principles of the Kingdom

5:1–7:29

THE KING EXTENDS THE MOSAIC LAW (Chapter 5)

1. **The Sermon on the Mount—the principles of the "kingdom of heaven"**

   Matthew records the Sermon on the Mount in greater detail than anyone else, devoting to it the whole of chapters 5-7. In this matchless address our Lord Jesus Christ presents the principles of the kingdom of heaven. Six times in these three chapters, including five occurrences in chapter five, Jesus speaks directly of the "kingdom of heaven," using that exact phrase. In addition he makes general reference to the kingdom several more times. However, the Lord's words are applicable to Christians during this dispensation and should never be thought of as having application only to the Twelve or to those living during the Millennium. They apply to us as well for three reasons.

First, he addressed his words to those who know God as their Father, and we do (e.g., 5:16, 45, 48; 6:1, 4, 6). Second, he spoke to citizens of the kingdom, and we are that in a mystical sense (Colossians 1:13).

Third, he gave this sermon in great detail, which we would not expect if it were to have no application to us.

2. The persons addressed (5:1-2; 7:28-29)

Jesus begins by addressing his disciples but concludes his speech to the multitude. Moreover, in the early part of the sermon he discusses matters appropriate for his own. This continues to 7:12, where he states what has come to be known as the Golden Rule, which he calls a summary of the teaching of the Old Testament Law and Prophets. It is also a summary of his sermon up to that point. Consider such statements as these: "You are the salt of the earth" (5:13); "You are the light of the world" (5:14); "that you may be the children of your Father" (5:45); and other expressions indicating that his hearers are disciples. Note, however, that we find nothing of this sort after 7:12. In the remainder of the sermon he preaches the Gospel; and when he refers to God in 7:21, he says not "your Father" but "my Father." He is evidently addressing the mixed crowd that gathered.

3. The Beatitudes (5:3–12)

If we regard verses 10–12 as a unit, since all three verses deal with the blessedness of those who are persecuted, there are eight Beatitudes in all. Each one comes either directly or indirectly from the Old Testament. Jesus is gathering together a number of items from Old Testament Scripture and arranging them in order at the start of his sermon. Note how he relates these considerations to the kingdom of heaven. He mentions that kingdom in the first and last of the Beatitudes (vv. 3, 10). The following list shows the relationship of the Beatitudes to Old Testament verses:

The poor in spirit, Psalm 51:17; Isaiah 57:15.
Those who mourn, Isaiah 61:2–3.
The meek, Psalm 37:11.
Those who hunger and thirst after righteousness, Psalm 37:11.
Those who are merciful, Psalm 18:25.
The pure in heart, Psalm 24:3–5.

References to peacemakers being being called the children of God are found in Isaiah 9:6–7, where the prophetic reference is, of course, to Christ, the Son who is the Prince of Peace. References to those persecuted for righteousness' sake are found in Daniel 3:19, 24–25. In most, if not all of these Beatitudes, Jesus adds to the new idea that such persons are "blessed," or "happy."

4. Citizenship in the kingdom (vv. 13–16)

After delivering the Beatitudes, the Lord speaks of citizenship in the kingdom. He characterizes the citizens—

namely, his immediate disciples and, by extension, all true Christians—as "the salt of the earth" (v. 13) and "the light of the world" (vv. 14–16).

Salt preserves from corruption; light illuminates. Hence, Christians are in the world to preserve it in some measure from corruption and to shed the light of divine truth in the darkness of this sinful world. This we can do in two ways: by the testimony of our lips and by the testimony of our lives.

Note the object of our light in verse 16.

5. Warnings in connection with citizenship in the kingdom (vv. 19-20)

First, the Lord warns that those who *were* citizens will occupy either a low or a high position in the kingdom, according to how they have performed the duties of the Law and instructed others in those duties (v. 19). Then he warns all his hearers that a certain kind of righteousness is required for *entrance into* the kingdom (v. 20). It must be a righteousness superior to that of the Scribes and Pharisees. This is a perfect righteousness, the righteousness of God, which is Christ himself. See Roman 10:1–4 and 2 Corinthians 5:21.

7. These warnings illustrated (vv. 21-48)

From this point to the end of the chapter, Jesus amplifies what he stated in verse 20. This he does by dealing successively with five items of Old Testament Law, showing the standards of the kingdom as far as keeping the Law is concerned. In each instance he goes beyond the mere letter of the Law and insists that there must be an observance of the spirit of the Law as well.

a. The sixth commandment (vv. 21–26)

As to murder, Jesus quotes the Law, "You shall not kill" (Exod. 20:13). And if you *want* to kill or if you are angry with your brother without cause, he says you have broken the spirit of the Law. He urges reconciliation with a brother before worshipping God (vv. 23–24) as well as with an adversary before filing a lawsuit (vv. 25–26).

b. The seventh commandment (vv. 27–32)

Next, he takes up the matter of sexual purity. Quoting the seventh commandment from Exodus 20:14, he says, "You shall not commit adultery." Even if a man merely *wants* to do so, he has broken the spirit of the commandment (v. 28). This leads him to discuss two related matters. First, he mentions the importance of excluding from life anything that might lead to sin (v. 29–30). In this connection Jesus refers to "hell," not Hades, the place of departed souls, but Gehenna, the place of burning.

Second, he speaks about divorce, saying the only proper cause is fornication (v. 31–32).

c. The matter of oaths (vv. 33–37)

The Lord Jesus repeats the prohibition against taking the name of God in vain (Exod. 20:7; Lev. 19:12) this way: "You shall not forswear yourself, but shall perform unto the Lord your oaths" (v. 33). He carries the prohibition further saying that we are not to take any oath, but to let our spoken word, yes or no, be sufficient (vv. 34–37).

d. The question of retaliation (vv. 38–42)

According to the Law, it was perfectly proper to require "an eye for eye, tooth for tooth," as stated in Exodus 21:24 (v. 38). But Jesus says we are not to retaliate but to forgive and be generous. We are not to exact justice but be gracious (vv. 39–42). All of this reminds us of the statement in John 1:17: "The law was given by Moses, but grace and truth came by Jesus Christ."

e. *Concerning love (vv. 43–48)*

Finally, Jesus comes to the root of the whole matter—love. He quotes from the Law, as stated in Leviticus 19:18: "You shall love your neighbor."

The part about hating enemies was added by certain rabbinical teachers, it seems, and is not found in Scripture. In introducing this question, Jesus says, "You have heard that it has been said" (v. 43). He not only condemned the unscriptural addition but extended the scriptural command to include love for an enemy as well. Seek their welfare, he says; pray for them. In so doing you shall show yourselves to be true children of your heavenly Father, for he sends his sunshine and his rain on good and bad alike.

8. Likeness to the heavenly Father—the believer's aim in the daily life (v. 48)

Now comes the statement toward which Jesus had been driving from the very start of his sermon. We are to be perfect, as perfect as is our heavenly Father. We may fail, and we do very often, but likeness to him should always be our aim. We *profess* to be children of God. If we truly believe, we *are* children of God. Hence, we are to *act the part* in our daily living.

THE KING DISCUSSES RIGHTEOUSNESS AND THE KINGDOM (Chapter 6)

In this section of the sermon, Jesus makes two main points: do good in secret (vv. 1–18) and put your treasure in heaven (vv. 19–34).

1. Doing good in secret (vv. 1–18)

The Lord gives a basic exhortation then follows it with three examples. He states the exhortation in the first half of verse 1; the reason, in the latter half. We are not to practice our righteousness (NASB) for the eyes of other people. If we do, we forfeit our heavenly Father's reward.

a. Almsgiving (vv. 2-4)

The first example Jesus cites is that of almsgiving. When we give help to those in need, we must not do it ostentatiously so others will see and give us credit (v. 2). Rather, we are to do it privately, for the eyes of God alone; this will earn his reward (vv. 3–4).

b. Prayer (vv. 5-15)

The second example is that of prayer. Christ warns about making a display of our praying (v. 5), and then recommends secret prayer, which God will reward (v. 6). He cautions too against useless repetitions in prayer, as though God were ignorant of our needs and must be reminded and impressed by repeated petitions (vv. 7–8).

Immediately following this warning, he gives a pattern for prayer (vv. 9–13). This is customarily called "The Lord's Prayer," though perhaps it would be more accurately called "The Disciples' Prayer." This prayer is not necessarily to be repeated word for word. It is only a pattern of prayer.

First, there is invocation and worship, which is the proper way to begin prayer (v. 9). Following this, there is petition for the glory of God (v. 10). Then there is petition for the blessing of the persons praying (vv. 11–13.)

Two petitions that are rather difficult to understand are found in verses 12–13.

With regard to the first difficulty, "Forgive us our debts, as we forgive our debtors," the Lord himself gives us the explanation. In verses 14 and 15 he says that our heavenly Father will not forgive us if we fail to forgive others who trespass against us. This does not refer to the forgiveness that reserves us a place in an undeserved heaven rather than in a deserved hell. We know this from many other texts, such as John 3:16; 5:24; 6:47; Acts 16:31 and Romans 10:9–10. In such scriptures, forgiveness does not depend on our doing anything, such as forgiving others, but solely on the principle of faith. Those who have already been forgiven in the sense mentioned above are children of God (observe "Our Father" in v. 9, "your heavenly Father" in v. 14, and "your Father" in v. 15) and are required to forgive others. When they do so they can expect their heavenly Father to forgive them in the sense of removing all barriers to happy fellowship in the family of God. The subject is discussed more fully in 1 John 1:5–10.

With regard to the second difficulty, "Lead us not into temptation, but deliver us from evil [or 'from the evil one']," presumably what the Lord means is that we are to pray that God will never act like Satan and lead a child of God into temptation but will be unlike Satan and provide a way of escape. In regard to leading us into temptation, James 1:13 says this is something God never does. As to the second, 1 Corinthians 10:13 says this is something God always does. Jesus tells us to pray for these things—that is, to consciously cast ourselves on God who always acts on these principles.

c. Fasting (vv. 16-18)

The third example of doing good in secret is that of fasting. The Lord's teaching on this follows the same principle as previously stated: our fasting should be done for God, not others, lest we lose our reward. If we fast, we are to do so for his sake and for his approval alone.

2. Treasure in heaven (vv. 19-34)

The Lord contrasts treasure in heaven with treasure on earth and assures us that, if we put first things first, he will provide for earthly necessities.

a. Treasures on earth or treasures in heaven—which will it be? (vv. 19-21)

We are not to amass treasures on earth for two reasons: (1) we may lose them (v. 19); (2) they will cause us to focus our attention on earth rather than on heaven.

God or mammon—whom shall we serve? (vv. 22-24)

We are exhorted to have a single purpose. That is, we are not to try to carry water on both shoulders. There must be no compromise between light and darkness, or good and evil. We are to make up our minds which master we are going to serve, God or mammon (i.e., riches).

c. "Be anxious for nothing"—Seek first the kingdom of God . . ." (vv. 25-34)

In the remainder of chapter 6, Jesus applies the principle stated in verse 24. Since we cannot serve both God and mammon, he urges us to serve God. We are not to be anxious regarding food and clothing (v. 25 NASB). Life is more important than the food that sustains it, and the body than the clothes it wears (v. 25). Furthermore, God makes provision for the fowls and the flowers, and we are much more important than they (vv. 26-29). Hence, he will certainly provide for us, his children (v. 30). For this reason, we are not to be anxious about material necessities (vv. 31-32, NASB). Rather, we are to seek first the kingdom of God and the righteousness of God. If we do this, the material necessities will be supplied (vv. 33-34). This puts no premium on idleness or laziness, but merely puts spiritual things before material.

THE KING CONCLUDES HIS SERMON (Chapter 7)

It is well to divide this chapter into two parts: the first consists of the remainder of the Lord's words to his disciples (vv. 1-12); the second, his appeal to the multitude in the rest of the chapter.

1. The Lord's concluding words to his disciples (vv. 1-12)

a. The matter of judging (vv. 1-6)

Continuing his address to his disciples, Jesus urges them—and us—not to judge others. As we judge, we shall be judged (vv. 1-2). If we are harsh or censorious, others—and perhaps God himself—will be harsh or censorious with us. Furthermore, we must be careful lest we criticize some small fault in a brother, when we ourselves are guilty of some flagrant fault (vv. 3–5). Again, we must be careful to use discrimination with regard to holy things and not carelessly display them before those who have no taste for spiritual truths (v. 6).

b. "Ask . . . seek . . . knock" (vv. 7–11).

Jesus urges that we "ask," "seek," and "knock" (vv. 7–8). If we do, we will certainly receive, find, and be invited in. He is speaking of asking our heavenly Father for his blessings (v. 11) and assuring that God will certainly give good things to his children who ask for them, since even sinful people do that much (vv. 9–11).

c. "The Golden Rule"—the climax and summary of the Sermon on the Mount (v. 12)

The Lord summarizes his entire message to his disciples in this verse, and in so doing he summarizes "the law and the prophets" as well. He says we are to do all that the Old Testament instructs us to do in connection with our duties to God and to our hearts, in love, observing not merely the letter but the spirit as well, and seeking the welfare of others just as we want them to seek our welfare.

2. The Lord's appeal to the multitude (vv. 13–27)

From verse 13 on, the Lord appeals to the multitude to take the way of life and build honestly and wisely, upon himself and his teachings, for eternity.

a. The narrow gate and the narrow way (vv. 13-14)

First, he exhorts them to choose the narrow gate and the narrow way so that spiritual life may be obtained. Truth is narrow; righteousness is restricting. If a person would have life, he or she must seek truth and righteousness. Christ is both. (See John 14:6; 1 Corinthians 1:30; and 2 Corinthians 5:21.)

b. Warning against false prophets and false servants (vv. 15-23)

We are to beware of wolves disguised as sheep (v. 15). The best way to discern them is by examining their fruits—their lives and the results of their ministry. Just as every tree is known by its fruit, so is every prophet or leader in spiritual things (vv. 16-20). As to false servants, the Lord stresses the importance of reality as opposed to mere profession. In other words, it is what a man is and does that counts, not what he professes (vv. 21-23). Some may even call him "Lord," and refer to "prophecies" and perform "miracles" in his name (vv. 21-22); yet those who have not done the will of the heavenly Father (v. 21) will hear God say to them those terrible words: "I never knew you: depart from me, you who work iniquity" (v. 23).

c. "A wise man" and "a foolish man" (vv. 24-27)

Finally, in a profound analogy, Jesus tells the stories of two men—one wise and one foolish. The wise man built his house on a rock (v. 24), and when the floods and wind came it weathered the raging storm (v. 25). The foolish man built his house on the sand (v. 26). So, said Jesus, is "every one who hears these sayings of mine." He who heeds and does them is wise—his house will stand (v. 24).

He who hears but does them not is foolish—his house will fall (v. 26).

Thus Jesus brings his incomparable sermon to a close.

The people are astonished at his teaching because he taught them, not as the scribes—merely citing the Law and the prophets—but with an authority they had never observed in any other (vv. 28–29).

5

The King Presents His Credentials

8:1–10:42

THE KING PERFORMS MANY MIRACLES (Chapter 8)

In chapter 8 our Lord performs a succession of varied miracles. One is the cleansing of a leper, another the curing of a handicapped man, a third the reduction of a fever. Another shows his mastery over nature, and still another his control over demons.

Jesus cleanses a leper (vv. 1-4)

After delivering the Sermon on the Mount, Jesus comes down the mountainside and is followed by great crowds of people. A leper appears, worships him, and states faith in Jesus' power to heal but questions his willingness. "Lord," he says, "if you will, you can make me clean" (v. 2). Jesus immediately reassures him of his willingness and, vindicating the man's faith, cleanses him of his leprosy (v. 3). Jesus cautions the man not to publish the cure and sends him to the priest in accordance with the Law of Moses (v. 4). (See Leviticus 14:1-32.)

2. Jesus heals the centurion's servant of palsy (vv. 5-13)

In Capernaum a Roman military officer appeals to Jesus for the healing of his servant (vv. 5-6). The Lord promises to go and heal him (v. 7), but the centurion protests that it is unnecessary for Jesus to go to him (vv. 8-9). He feels unworthy to have the Lord in his house and suggests that Jesus need only speak the word and the servant will be healed. Jesus commends this officer for his great faith (v. 10). Then he makes a significant statement regarding the inclusion of Gentiles in the kingdom of heaven (vv. 11-12). He says the kingdom is for those who believe, not for those who have a certain ancestry. The Lord now speaks the word, and immediately the servant is healed (v. 13).

3. Jesus heals Peter's mother-in-law of fever (vv. 14-15)

Following this, Jesus goes to Peter's house and finds Peter's mother-in-law sick with a fever. He touches her hand, the fever leaves her, and she rises and serves them.

4. Jesus casts out many demons, and heals "all that were sick" (vv. 16–17)

Later that day many are brought to Jesus, some demon-possessed, some physically ill. He heals them all in accordance with a prophecy from Isaiah (vv. 16–17; cf. Isa. 53:4).

Next Jesus crosses the Sea of Galilee (v. 18).

In the foregoing instances, Jesus' cures are characterized by two striking features: they are instantaneous and they are complete.

5. The cost of discipleship (vv. 19–22)

During an interlude the Lord deals with two men concerning the cost of discipleship. To a scribe who says, "Master, I will follow you wherever you go," Jesus says, You must be content, then, to be a homeless pilgrim (vv. 19–20). To another, who wants to stay with his father till he dies, Jesus says, Leave your father, if necessary, but follow me (vv. 21–22).

6. Jesus calms the tempest (vv. 23–27)

The next miracle concerns nature. During a violent storm at sea the Lord is asleep. As waves dash over the ship, the disciples awaken Jesus, saying, "Lord, save us, we perish" (vv. 23–25). Jesus reproves them for their small faith and then calms the winds and the sea, astounding his disciples. They say to one another, "What kind of man is this, that even the winds and the sea obey him!" (vv. 26–27). Apparently his ability to control nature is even more remarkable to them than his ability to control disease and demons.

7. Jesus delivers two demon-possessed men (vv. 28–34)

In the final miracle in this chapter two fierce, demon-possessed men meet Jesus as he is passing through the Gadarnes (NASB). The demons in the men recognize Jesus as the Son of God and cry out, asking if he has come to torment them before their time (vv. 28–29). Evidently they know they are to be punished in hell (see Matthew 25:41) and are apprehensive about some preliminary torment. The demons, expecting to be cast out of the two men, request that they be allowed to enter a herd of swine feeding some distance away (vv. 30–31). Jesus gives his consent, and the whole herd plunges down into the sea and drown. The swineherds rush to the city and tell the owners of the swine what has happened. Then the people of the city come out to meet Jesus. Instead of falling at his feet and acknowledging him as the Christ, however, they beg him to leave their part of the country (vv. 32–34). Such are the hearts of unbelievers and such is the bitterness of unbelief!

THE KING ESTABLISHES HIS DEITY (Chapter 9)

1. Jesus proves his power to forgive sin—the healing of the palsied man (vv. 1–8)

The first incident in this chapter is of prime importance. Jesus returns to Capernaum (v. 1), and a palsied man is brought to him. The Lord determines to make this a test case. Seeing their faith—presumably that of the men who carried him and the palsied man himself—he says to the sick man, "Son, be of good cheer; your sins are forgiven"

(v. 2). Some of the scribes, hearing this, say to themselves, "This man blasphemes" (v. 3). Since only God can forgive sins, there are just two possibilities here. Either he is God, and thus has the power and authority to forgive sins; or he is a fraud and therefore a blasphemer. The scribes assume the latter. Knowing this, Jesus asks, "Which is easier, to say, 'Your sins be forgiven,' or to say, 'Arise and walk'?" (vv. 4–5). The point Jesus is making is that anyone with the power to say the second statement has the authority to say the first. The proof of the matter lies in what follows. To prove that he possesses the authority to forgive sins—and is therefore God in human flesh—he puts the matter to the test. Addressing the palsied man, he tells him to rise, take up his bed, and go home. If the man is unable to do so, the scribes are right. If he does it, Jesus has proved his point. His claim to have the authority to forgive sins—that is, his claim to deity—has been honored by God in the man's miraculous cure. No wonder, then, that the multitude marvel and glorify God when the miracle takes place before their eyes (vv. 6–8).

In all this, Jesus is presenting his credentials, thus proving that he is indeed the Christ, the Messiah of Old Testament prophecy, the Son of God.

2. The call of Matthew the publican (v. 9; cf. vv. 10–13)

After this demonstration of his deity, Jesus calls another of his disciples, Matthew the publican. Mark and Luke call this man Levi and state that he was the host of a dinner that follows (v. 10), which is attended by many publicans and sinners. The Pharisees ask Jesus' disciples about this (v. 11), and Jesus replies that this is in accordance with his purpose for coming to earth (vv. 12–13). "I am not come to call the righteous," he says, "but sinners to repentance."

3. The question about fasting answered by three illustrations (vv. 14–17)

The disciples of John the Baptist question Jesus as to why his disciples do not fast. Jesus answers with three illustrations: (1) the companions of a bridegroom do not fast so long as the bridegroom is with them; (2) no one mends an old garment with a piece of new cloth; and (3) no one puts new wine in an old wineskin. It is impossible, Jesus is saying, to mix the law, which John represents and of which fasting is a part, and grace, which is represented by Christ himself.

4. A double miracle—Jesus raises the dead and heals the sick (vv. 18–26)

The Lord goes to restore life to a little girl who has died (vv. 18–19). Mark and Luke tell us that she is the daughter of Jairus.

On the way to Jairus's house, Jesus heals a woman who has suffered for twelve years with a blood disorder (vv. 20–22). He says to the woman, "Your faith has made you whole."

The restoration of Jairus's daughter to life is the only miracle of resurrection Jesus performed during his public ministry that Matthew records (vv. 23–26).

5. Jesus gives sight to the blind and cast out a demon (vv. 27–34)

After this, the Lord performs two more miracles: (1) he gives sight to two blind men (vv. 27–31) and (2) he casts out a demon that has made its victim unable to speak (vv. 32–34). In the former case, Jesus restores their sight on the basis of their faith in him (v. 29). Of the latter, the Pharisees make a blasphemous accusation: "He casts out devils through the prince of the devils" (v. 34).

6. The Lord Jesus in Galilee—"teaching . . . preaching . . . healing" (vv. 35–38)

The chapter closes with a brief statement about the Lord's activity on behalf of the people. He visits all the cities and villages of the area, teaching in the synagogues, preaching the Gospel of the kingdom, and healing all sorts of sickness and disease among the people (v. 35). But as he looks upon the multitudes, the seriousness of their sinful condition reaches his heart. He sees them as scattered, fainting sheep without a shepherd (v. 36). This leads him to say to his disciples, "The harvest truly is plenteous, but the laborers are few" (v. 37). In view of this fact, he urges them to pray that the Lord "will send forth laborers into his harvest" (v.38).

This is an excellent prayer for us to pray, one that may well result in an answer that sends us out as laborers into the harvest field of souls, as it did the disciples.

THE KING ORDAINS AND COMMISSIONS THE TWELVE (Chapter 10)

The Twelve commissioned and sent forth (vv. 1–15)

The Lord calls his twelve disciples apart from the rest and gives them authority over unclean spirits and all sorts of sickness and disease (v. 1). A list of the twelve follows (vv. 2–4).

Before sending them out he instructs them regarding objectives, duties, and support (vv. 5–15). As to objectives, they are to go only to "the lost sheep of the house of Israel" (vv. 5–6). As to duties, they are to preach the kingdom of heaven, heal the sick, raise the dead, cleanse the lepers, and cast out demons. Their message is similar to that of John the Baptist and, later, of Jesus. What they have received as a gift, they are to pass on to other Jews as a gift (vv. 7–8). As to support, they are to accept food and shelter from those who receive them and their message (vv. 9–11). Furthermore, those to whom they preach are to be held responsible for receiving their message (vv. 12–15).

2. Persecution of the Lord's messengers foretold (vv. 16–23)

The next few verses seem to refer not only to the present situation but also to the preaching of the Gospel of the kingdom just before the Lord's return. Although it is clear that the verses specifically have Jews in view, in principle they apply also to the preaching of the Gospel of grace in our day.

Note "councils," and "synagogues" (v. 17); "them and the Gentiles" (v. 18); "cities of Israel" (v. 23). In other words, persecution is to be expected as a consequence of preaching the message of God.

3. Discipleship and its demands (vv. 24–39)

The Lord takes up six items concerning discipleship and its demands. The first is that of *reproach* (vv. 24–25). The disciple of the Lord Jesus is to expect the same sort of treatment as his Master or Teacher. Next comes the matter of *witness* (vv. 26–27). We are to give our testimony publicly and without fear. After this, Jesus speaks of *martyrdom* (vv. 28–31). We are not to fear it. It can come only with our heavenly Father's permission. Fourth, the Lord takes up the contrasting points of *confession and denial* (vv. 32–33). Our confession of him before others will bring his confession of us before his father. Our denial of him before men will result in his denial of us before his Father. Then he speaks of *family strife* (vv. 34–37). We must love him more than we love our closest relatives. The sixth and last item concerns *the cross a disciple must bear* (vv. 38–39). We must follow Christ, though losing our lives for his sake. Thus we shall find life in the best sense.

4. The promise of reward for those who receive the Lord's own (vv. 40–42)

There are rewards for receiving those who belong to Christ. Whoever receives a disciple receives Christ and the Father (v. 40). Receiving a prophet or a righteous man brings a prophet's or a righteous man's reward (v. 41). Even so small a thing as giving a drink of cold water to one of the Lord's little ones, merely in the name of a disciple, will bring a sure reward (v. 42).

6

The King Declares His Rejection

11:1–12:50

THE KING PROCLAIMS THE FACT OF HIS REJECTION (11:1-19)

1. **Jesus' answer to the imprisoned John—a Messianic claim (vv. 1-6)**

   After commanding his twelve disciples (chap. 10), Jesus proceeds to teach and preach in the cities of Galilee (v. 1). John the Baptist, in prison, hearing about the works and miracles of Jesus, sends two of his disciples to find out if Jesus is indeed the Christ (vv. 2-3). The reason for John's doubt was probably his imprisonment. If Jesus could perform miracles, why hadn't he released his faithful herald John the Baptist? John was confused as to why he remained in prison for preaching repentance and heralding the King. When the messengers come, Jesus tells them to return to John and tell him what they have heard and seen: The blind receiving sight, the lame walking, lepers being cleansed, the deaf hearing, the dead being raised, and the poor having the Gospel preached to them (vv. 4–6). John, familiar with the Book of Isaiah, which predicted his own ministry (Isa. 40: 3–4), will undoubtedly recall its prophecy that when God comes, miracles like these would occur (Isa. 35:4–6).

2. **Jesus' testimony to John—the messenger of the King—another Messianic claim (vv. 7—11)**

When the disciples of John leave, Jesus addresses the multitude and announces to them that he and John have both been rejected already by the people as a whole (vv. 7–19). First, he asks them why they went out into the wilderness to see John (vv. 7–9a). Then he states his own high estimate of John: "More than a prophet," equal to the greatest of God's messengers among men. Yet, in position and privilege, he is inferior to the least in the kingdom of heaven (vv. 9b–11). John, then, was not in the Kingdom, and to be of the Kingdom is a greater privilege than to be of the Law.

3. **Opposition to the Kingdom as evidenced by the rejection of John and the Kingdom.**

From the days of John, the Kingdom had been suffering violence (v.12). This suggests that opposition to the Kingdom had been evident and violent ever since John had started to proclaim it, or at least since he had been imprisoned. Then Jesus says that John is the last of the prophets under the Law (v. 13) and, furthermore, that John was or might have been the fulfillment, if the Jews had believed, of the prophecy of Malachi 4:5 regarding the coming of Elijah (vv. 14–15).

4. **The climax of the King's announcement of the rejection of the Kingdom (vv. 16–19)**

Jesus compares that generation of Jews to children in the marketplace to whom their companions call saying, "We have piped unto you, and you have not danced"(vv. 16–17). John had proclaimed the Kingdom to them solemnly, distantly, aloof (v. 18). Their reaction to him had been: "He has a demon" (NASB). Jesus himself had proclaimed the Kingdom to them happily, intimately, mixing with the people; and their reaction to him was: "Behold a man gluttonous, and a winebibber, a friend of publicans and sinners" (v. 19). But, said he, wisdom is justified, or demonstrated, by her children, or works.

THE KING CONDEMNS THREE GALILEAN CITIES (11:20–24)

Having plainly stated the fact of the rejection of the Kingdom; of John, its herald; and of himself, its King—the Lord proceeds to condemn certain cities of Galilee in which he had performed most of his great miracles. The reason for his condemnation? Though they had heard the message of repentance and had seen his miracles, they did not repent (v. 20). First, Chorazin and Bethsaida are condemned as being more guilty than Tyre and Sidon, two wicked Gentile cities north of Galilee (vv. 21–22).

Then proud Capernaum is found to be more blameworthy than wicked Sodom of Abraham's day (vv. 23–24).

THE KING INVITES THE HEAVY-LADEN TO HIMSELF (11:25-30)

1. Jesus' prayer of thanksgiving (vv. 25-26)

We have first a prayer of thanksgiving that his Father had hidden these things—these spiritual truths—from the wise and prudent, and to reveal them to babes. That is to say, God hides his truth from those who seek it through their own worldly wisdom but reveals it to those who make no pretence of any wisdom of their own and are willing to humbly learn from God what he has to reveal to them. (See 1 Corinthians 1:18–21; 2:6–10.)

2. The Lord's great invitation (vv. 27-30)

The basis of the great invitation is stated first (v. 27). The Father has delivered all things into his hands; and since no one knows the Son but the Father, and no one knows the Father but the Son and those to whom the Son will reveal him, he invites those who want to know the Father to come to him for the revelation. The invitation itself comes next, perhaps the most wonderful invitation in all human history (vv. 28–29a). Those who labor under a heavy load of sin, and of legal ceremonialism because of sin, are invited to come to him, with the assurance that he will give rest. Then, having received the rest of soul that only he can give, the believing disciple is asked to take Christ's yoke upon him, for service, and learn of him. His yoke is found to be easy, and his burden light (vv. 29b–30).

THE KING AND THE SABBATH (12:1-14)

"The Lord of the sabbath" and his defense of his disciples concerning so-called "sabbath-breaking" (vv. 1-8)

The events of chapter 12 show how true the statement was, in chapter 11, that the Jews had rejected the King and his kingdom. First, there is the question of the observance of the Sabbath day. Jesus' disciples, hungry, pluck the grain and eat it on the Sabbath (v. 1). The Pharisees complain that they are breaking the Sabbath (v. 2). Jesus defends them (vv. 3-8) using three arguments. First, David and his men ate the shewbread, which it was unlawful for any but the priests to eat (vv. 3-4). See 1 Samuel 21:4-6. Circumstances made this a proper thing for them to do, since David was at this time a rejected king, fleeing from Saul. Again, the Temple priests perform certain necessary tasks on the Sabbath, thus "breaking the Sabbath," but are blameless (v. 5). In fact, the Law itself specified certain tasks for the Sabbath day. See Numbers 28:9-10. Once more, Jesus says that he himself is greater than the Temple (v. 6); that as Son of Man he is Lord of the Sabbath (v. 8); and that, if these Pharisees had known the meaning of that Old Testament pronouncement, given in Hosea 6:6, "For I desired mercy and not sacrifice," they would not have condemned the guiltless disciples (v. 7).

Jesus' healing of the withered hand on the Sabbath; the Jews' council to destroy him (vv. 9-14)

Following this exchange, Jesus goes into the local synagogue (v. 9). A man with a withered hand is there, and the Lord is asked whether it is lawful to heal on the

Sabbath. The Pharisees are looking for proof that Jesus teaches it is right to "break the Sabbath" under certain conditions (v. 10). Jesus goes beyond merely answering their question and actually "breaks the Sabbath" himself by *curing* the man. Jesus says, "You will lift a sheep out of a pit on the Sabbath, will you not? Is a man not better than a sheep?" (vv. 11–12). Then he heals the man's hand (v. 13). The Pharisees, incensed, hold a council, and plan his destruction (v. 14). But not before Jesus has both taught and proved that it is lawful to do good on the Sabbath day (v. 12).

THE KING AND BLASPHEMY (12:15–32)

1. The fulfillment of Isaiah 42:1-7 concerning Jehovah's Servant (vv. 15–21)

In this part of the chapter, the Pharisees' hatred for Jesus reaches a high point, and Jesus brands it as blasphemy. Jesus, knowing they are plotting to destroy him, goes elsewhere, followed by great multitudes. He heals all their sick and instructs them to not make him known (vv. 15–16). This fulfills the prophecy in Isaiah 42: 1–7 regarding Jehovah's Servant, who was not to strive or cry or break a bruised reed, and in whose name the Gentiles were to trust (vv. 17–21). He was to be gentle, loving, kind, at his first coming, avoiding strife and showing grace.

2. The unpardonable sin—blasphemy against the Holy Spirit (vv. 22–32)

Something occurs that brings from his gracious lips a scathing denunciation, not on his own behalf but on behalf of the Holy Spirit.

A man both blind and dumb, possessed of a demon, is brought to Jesus, and he heals him, giving the man both sight and speech (v. 22). The people's reaction is to wonder whether this is not the Son of David (v. 23). But the Pharisees think otherwise. They say, "This man casts out demons only by Beelzebub the ruler of the demons" (v. 24 NASB).

Jesus does three things. First, he reads their thoughts (v. 25a). This reveals his supernatural power.

Second, he shows the foolishness of their reasoning (vv. 25b–30). If he is casting out demons by the power of the prince of demons, as they say he is, then Satan is casting out Satan, something he would be entirely too wise to do, as that would break up his kingdom (vv. 25–26). Furthermore, even if he were casting out demons by Beelzebub, how about their children, presumably meaning his disciples (v. 27)? See also Matthew 10:1, 8; Luke 10:1, 17. The only other alternative is that he is casting out demons by the Spirit of God, in which case the Kingdom of God has come to them (v. 28). He is curbing the power of Satan by casting out these demons and will proceed to destroy his kingdom (v. 29). There is no room for neutrality. People are either for the Lord or against him, either favorable to the Kingdom of God or to the kingdom of Satan (v. 30).

Third, he brands them as blasphemers (vv. 31–32). Jesus says the Pharisees have been blaspheming the Holy Spirit, which is something unforgivable either in this age or in the next (vv. 31–32).

THE KING AND REALITY (12:33–50)

As the chapter closes, four items are presented that emphasize the distinction between hypocrisy and reality.

1. **"Out of the abundance of the heart the mouth speaks" (vv. 33-37)**

   The first of these four items consists of the words of Jesus. Here he speaks of trees and people. As the fruit of a tree reveals the kind of tree it is, so people, by their words, reveal the kind they are (vv. 33-35). People are sometimes hypocritical and say things they do not mean. Of all such words they must give account in the day of judgment (vv. 36-37).

2. **The sign of Jonah—prophetic of Jesus' resurrection (vv. 38-42)**

   The second item has to do with the request of some of the scribes and Pharisees for a sign. Jesus characterizes such as still seek a sign, or credentials, from him—after all that have already been given—as "an evil and adulterous generation" (v. 39a). That is, they are wickedly and hypocritically seeking a sign. No further sign is to be given except the sign of Jonah (vv. 39b, 40). This would be the miraculous sign of his own resurrection after three days. Further more, this generation will be condemned by the men of Nineveh, who repented at the preaching of Jonah (v. 41); and by the queen of the south, the queen of Sheba, who traveled far to hear the wisdom of Solomon (v. 42). This generation did not repent; nor did it seek genuinely for words of wisdom, even though one greater than either Jonah or Solomon was in its midst.

3. **The peril of "this wicked generation" (vv. 43-45)**

   In his third reference to the hypocrisy of that generation, Jesus tells of an unclean spirit who leaves a man and, upon returning, finds the man with no spiritual interest whatever. He is rid of the evil spirit, but has nothing real and profitable in its place; he has no God. The evil spirit re-enters the man with seven others more wicked than himself, and the man is worse off than he was at the beginning. This hypocritical generation is like that man. With no God, and with no real desire for spiritual truth, these people are in grave danger of being possessed by Satan to a most vicious extent.

4. **The difference between real disciples and those who reject the Lord's claims to Messiahship (vv. 46–50)**

The final item has to do with a visit by Jesus' mother and brethren. They come "desiring to speak with him" (v. 46). Informed of their desire, he uses the occasion to point up the difference between those who are his disciples and those who are not (vv. 47–48). Indicating his disciples, he says, "Behold my mother and my brethren" (v. 49). "Whoever shall do the will of my father which is in heaven, the same is my brother, and sister, and mother" (v. 50). Thus he implies that those who have seen his credentials, have heard his teachings and his claims, and yet have failed to become his disciples, are resisting the will of God. They are hypocrites, with no real desire for God and his truth. They have rejected him and his kingdom.

7

The King Declares the Mysteries of the Kingdom

13:1–58

PARABLES AND EXPLANATIONS BY THE SEASIDE (13:1–35)

The bulk of this chapter is occupied with seven parables of the kingdom of heaven, together with the Lord's own explanation of three of them. In addition, this chapter explains the reasons for speaking in parables, an additional parable regarding instructed scribes, and a further record of Christ's rejection.

These seven parables were spoken by Jesus the same day (v. 1) as were his previous statements regarding the blasphemy of the Pharisees against the Holy Spirit (12:31–32) and his denunciation of that generation of Jews for their wickedness and hypocrisy (12:34, 39–45). Also, the first four parables were spoken to the multitudes by the seaside (vv. 1–3a) while the others were spoken to his disciples in the house (vv. 31ff.).

1. The parable of the sower (vv. 3b–9)

The first parable is that of the sower. The sower sows his seed, which is all of one kind, but it falls on four different types of ground: "wayside," "stony places," "among thorns," and "good ground." The fowls devour the seed that falls by the wayside; the sun scorches the seed that quickly springs up in stony places; the thorns choke the seed that falls among thorns; but the seed that falls into good ground brings forth abundant fruit. This parable is explained in verses 18–23.

2. "The mysteries of the kingdom of heaven" (vv. 10–17)

Following the first parable, the Lord explains to the disciples two reasons for speaking in parables (v. 11): (1) Those who have faith will be helped by these parables to understand the mysteries of the kingdom of heaven; (2) Those who have not faith will only be mystified by them.

In the Bible, a mystery is a truth kept secret in the councils of God. The mysteries of the kingdom of heaven are revealed in these parables for believers to receive and understand. Those who have faith receive revelations of truth, but those who are in unbelief have everything stripped from them (v. 12). The people generally are in unbelief and here they see, but do not perceive; they hear, but do not understand (v. 13). This is in fulfillment of the prophecy in Isaiah 6:9–10 (vv. 14–15). Then the Lord congratulates his disciples on their faith, for by it they see and hear truths denied to prophets and righteous men who lived before these "mysteries," or secrets, were revealed (vv. 16–17).

3. Jesus' explanation of the parable of the sower (vv. 18–23)

Next Jesus explains to his disciples the parable of the sower. "The word of the kingdom," or God's good news, is preached, or taught, and is heard by four different types of persons. The "wayside" hearer is one who does not understand the message. The devil comes and snatches it away before it makes any real impression (v. 19). The "stony places" hearer receives the message at once and with joy; but because there is no root, trouble or persecution soon causes the professer of faith to fall away (vv. 20–21, NASB). The hearer "among the thorns" soon becomes unfruitful because of worldly cares and earthly riches which deceive (v. 22). Fruit is yielded only in the case of the "good ground." This hearer understands the Word and yields abundant fruit (v. 23).

4. The parable of the wheat and the tares (vv. 24–30)

After this, Jesus speaks a second parable to the multitude—that of the wheat and tares. Here our Lord compares the kingdom of heaven to a situation in which a person sows good seed (v. 24). Stealthily, his enemy sows tares, or weeds, among the wheat (v. 25). When the wheat springs up, the tares appear also (v. 26). The man's servants report the matter, and he tells them it is the work of an enemy. Then the servants ask if they should pull up the tares (vv. 27–28). He says no because they might pull up some of the wheat also (v. 29). Both are to be allowed to grow together till harvest time, when he will instruct the reapers to gather the tares for burning and the wheat for storing in his barn (v. 30). This parable Jesus interprets for his disciples a little later.

5. The parable of the mustard seed (vv. 31–32)

In this parable a man sows a single grain of mustard seed, the least of all seeds. Though the seed is so small, the plant becomes very large, a tree in fact, so that the birds lodge in its branches. This, too, is compared to the kingdom of heaven.

Neither this parable, nor any of the next three, is explained by the Lord. But the key to the explanation of all is supplied by the Lord in his explanation of the first two.

The kingdom of heaven starts out as a very small and apparently insignificant thing, developing abnormally into a huge growth capable of supporting false teachers and preachers, representatives of the devil (see vv. 4–19), who desire support from the tree. This tree is the professing church—those who claim to be Christians. The professing church has grown to unnatural proportions by receiving into itself great numbers of persons who have no true faith and hence have not been born again.

6. The parable of the leaven (v. 33)

The remaining parable in this first group is that of the leaven. The kingdom of heaven is compared to a situation in which a woman hides leaven in three measures of meal till the whole is leavened. To understand this parable we need to consider the significance of leaven in the Bible. Similar to yeast, it was to be left out of bread eaten at the Passover and during the following week. See Exodus 12:8–15. In the Old Testament, it represents evil; and in the New Testament the Lord Jesus and the apostle Paul specifically use it to refer to evil, either in doctrine or in practice. See Matthew 16:6–12 and 1 Corinthians 5:6–8. Jesus is evidently prophesying that the professing church will eventually become permeated by evil or false doctrine, and perhaps also by evil or ungodly conduct and practice. All this has occurred and is true today.

7. Jesus' parables—a fulfillment of prophecy (vv. 34–35)

Our Lord's speaking in parables is in harmony with the statement made in the opening verses of Psalm 78.

PARABLES AND EXPLANATIONS IN THE HOUSE (13:36–52)

1. Jesus' explanation of "the parable of the tares" (vv. 36–43)

After sending the multitude away, Jesus goes into the house. His disciples come to him and ask for an explanation of the parable of the tares (v. 36). His explanation follows in verses 37 through 43. The sower of the good seed is the Son of Man (v. 37). Note how this differs from the parable of the sower. The field is the world of mankind. The good seed are the sons of the kingdom (NASB) and the tares are the sons of the wicked one, Satan (v. 38). Again, note how this parable differs from that of the sower. The enemy is the devil; the harvest, the end of the age—the present Christian age of grace—and the reapers are the angels (v. 39). At the end of this age, the Son of Man will send his angels, who will gather out of his Kingdom all things that offend and those who practice lawlessness. The angels will cast these false citizens of the Kingdom into a furnace of fire to suffer anguish (vv. 40–42). Then the true citizens, the righteous, shall shine forth as the sun in the Kingdom of their Father (v. 43).

2. The parable of the "treasure hid in a field" (v. 44)

In the fifth parable, the kingdom of heaven is compared to a situation in which a man finds treasure hid in a field. The man hides his discovery, joyfully sells all his possessions, and buys the field. This suggests that God the Father gave his beloved and only Son for the world to redeem Israel to himself. See Isaiah 43:1; Romans 11:26.

3. The parable of "the pearl of great price" (vv. 45–46)

In the sixth parable, the kingdom of heaven is compared to a merchant searching for quality pearls. When he finds one of great price, he sells all he has and buys that pearl. This suggests the glorious fact that our Lord Jesus Christ gave his all, even himself, to redeem the church to himself. See Ephesians 1:7; 5:25–27.

4. **The parable of the dragnet (vv. 47–50)**

The seventh parable compares the kingdom of heaven to a net, or dragnet, which, when cast into the sea, gathers fish of every sort (v. 47). When it is full, it is drawn to shore and the good fish are gathered into vessels and the bad thrown away (v. 48). This parable is explained by our Lord. At the end of the age, the angels will come and separate the wicked from the just, casting the former into the furnace of fire (vv. 49–50). Note the similarity between this parable and that of the wheat and the tares.

5. **The first four parables—a summary of the history of the professing church**

In the first four parables there is a progression in the degree to which evil affects the kingdom of heaven. In the parable of the sower, evil is on the *outside*, represented by the birds that take away the seed that falls by the wayside. In the parable of the tares, evil is *alongside*, the tares growing among or beside the wheat in the field. In the parable of the mustard seed, evil is *topside*, the birds lodging in the branches of the tree. And in the parable of the leaven, evil is *inside*, the leaven permeating the whole mass of dough.

The history of the professing church reveals the increasing effect of evil on it and influence over it. These four parables summarize the history of the professing church, the kingdom of heaven in this age.

6. **The significance of the last three parables**

The last three parables, spoken privately to the Lord's disciples, deal with three major points regarding the kingdom of heaven. First, the redemption of Israel; second, the redemption of the church; third, the segregation of professing believers from true believers at the end of this age.

7. The parable of the householder (vv. 51–52)

After speaking all these parables, Jesus asks his disciples whether they have understood everything. When they answer in the affirmative, he speaks an eighth parable to them (vv. 51–52). If they understand the kingdom of heaven, he implies, it is their duty to pass their knowledge on to others and to differentiate between the Kingdom and the Law.

UNBELIEF IN THE KING'S OWN COUNTRY (13:53–58)

Having finished all these parables, Jesus leaves for his own country. Going into their synagogue, he teaches them, and they are astonished at his wisdom and his miracles (vv. 53–54). Assuming he cannot be anyone unusual because they know his entire family, they are offended. That is, they stumble over the fact that they know him so well, and as a result they fail to discern who he really is (vv. 55–57a). Jesus comments that a prophet usually is honored on the outside, but not at home. Because of their unbelief, he does not do many mighty works in that city (vv. 57b–58).

8

The King Presents Additional Credentials

14:1–15:39

MARTYRDOM OF JOHN THE BAPTIST (14:1-12)

In Matthew 14–15 we have another group of miracles, reminding us of chapters 8–10. Before relating these, however, Matthew introduces some background, which forms the substance of this first section.

Herod the tetrarch—a son of the Herod of Matthew 2, and ruler, under Rome, of Galilee—hears of the fame of Jesus (14:1). A short while before, he had had John the Baptist beheaded, and he thinks Jesus may be John risen from the dead and performing miracles (14:2). Actually, John had not performed miracles (see John 10:41). The sordid story is then told of John's martyrdom (14:3–12). John had told Herod it was unlawful for him to have Herodias as his wife, since she had previously been married to his brother (half brother) Philip. For this reason, Herod had John arrested, bound, and imprisoned (14:3–4). He would have put him to death but the people generally regarded John as a prophet, so he was afraid (14:5). However, on Herod's birthday, Herodias' daughter—having danced before Herod and others, having pleased her foster father, and having been instructed beforehand by her mother—requested John's head on a platter (14:6–8). Herod reluctantly fulfills his oath, and John is beheaded (14:9–11). His disciples come, claim the body and bury it, and tell Jesus (14:12).

JESUS FEEDS MORE THAN FIVE THOUSAND (14:13–21)

Hearing of John's murder, Jesus crosses the Sea of Galilee to a desert place and is followed by a great multitude of people. When Jesus sees them, he heals the sick among them (14:13–14). Late that day, his disciples suggest that he send the people away so they may buy food for themselves (14:15). To their astonishment, Jesus says that is not necessary: "Give them to eat," he says. When they question him, saying they have only five loaves and two fishes, Jesus says, "Bring them to me" (14:16–18).

Jesus then multiplies that very small supply of food so that five thousand men, with women and children in addition, are fed and satisfied, with twelve baskets full of leftovers (14:19–21). This is the only miracle performed by our Lord, apart from his own resurrection, that is related by all four Gospel writers.

JESUS WALKS ON THE WATER (14:22–33)

Early the next morning Jesus performs another miracle, but this time only his disciples witness it. He sends them across the Sea of Galilee in a boat and he dismisses the multitude. Then he goes up a mountainside to pray alone, while his disciples struggle with a rough wind on the water (14:22–24). In the fourth watch, between three and six in the morning, Jesus approaches their boat, walking on the water. When they see him, thinking he is a ghost, they cry out in fear. Jesus immediately reassures them, saying, "Be of good cheer; it is I; be not afraid" (14:25–27). Peter, apparently not quite convinced yet proving his confidence in the Lord Jesus if it really is he, replies: "Lord, if it is you, tell me to come to you on the water" (14:28). Jesus responds with just one word: "Come." Peter steps down from the boat and starts toward Jesus on the water; but, seeing how the wind is making the water rough, he is afraid. Evidently he takes his eyes off Jesus to look at the water. Beginning to sink, he cries out: "Lord, save me" (14:29–30). Jesus catches him at once, saying: "Oh you of little faith, why did you doubt?" Then they get into the boat and the wind ceases (14:31–32).

Note the effect of all this on the disciples. They come and worship him, saying, "Truly, you are the Son of God" (14:33).

There really seem to be *four miracles* here. First, Jesus himself walks on the surface of the water. Second, he enables Peter to do likewise. Third, he saves Peter from sinking. Fourth, he makes the wind stop blowing.

JESUS HEALS MANY IN GENNESARET (14:34–36)

When they land at Gennesaret, and the men there find out who Jesus is, they send out into the entire countryside for all the sick folk, requesting that they just be allowed to touch the hem of Jesus' garment. "And as many as touched were made perfectly whole."

TRADITIONALISM VERSUS OBEDIENCE TO GOD (15:1–20)

Following the miracles of chapter 14, some of the scribes and Pharisees of Jerusalem come to Jesus and raise a question about tradition. "Why do your disciples transgress the tradition of the elders? for they do not wash their hands when they eat bread" (vv. 1–2). To this the Lord replies with a scathing denunciation, declaring that they themselves are doing something far worse. By their tradition they are transgressing, not some other tradition, but a commandment; and a commandment, not of men, but of God (v. 3). Then he cites an example. *God* had said: "Honor your father and mother," and "He who speaks evil of father or mother, let him be put to death" (v. 4 NASB, citing Exod. 20:12; 21:17). But the Pharisees twisted this and said that it was enough to dedicate to God money that would be used for the support of needy parents—that is, make it available for the use of the religious leaders. Thus they made the commandment of God of no effect (vv. 5–6). Then he cites Isaiah 29:13, branding them as hypocrites who worship God with their lips but not with their hearts, and who teach others the commandments of men as though they were the commands of God (vv. 7–9).

Next, calling the multitude, he explains that it is not what goes into the mouth, but that which comes out of the mouth, that defiles a person (vv. 10–11).

His disciples come to him and report that the Pharisees are offended by his saying (v. 12). Jesus brushes this aside with the assertion that these Pharisees are "blind leaders of the blind," and that, "if the blind lead the blind, both shall fall into the ditch" (vv. 13–14). In other words, it was no wonder they stumbled; they were blind to spiritual truth.

Peter speaks up and asks for an explanation (v. 15). Jesus explains that what goes into the mouth passes through the natural process of digestion and elimination, but the things that come out of the mouth proceed from the heart (vv. 16–18). A person is not defiled by eating with unwashed hands, but by the evil thoughts, deeds, and words that come out of the heart (vv. 19–20).

JESUS EXTENDS GRACE TO A WOMAN OF CANAAN (15:21–28)

The Lord goes north to the vicinity of Tyre and Sidon, along the Mediterranean Sea and beyond the confines of the Holy Land (v. 21). Here a woman of Canaan, a Gentile, pleads for the deliverance of her daughter from demon possession (v. 22). Jesus seems to be harsh and unsympathetic with this woman, but actually he is drawing out an expression of her superb faith. At first, he ignores her. But she persists until his disciples ask him to send her away because she is annoying them (v. 23). Evidently, they want him to heal her to rid them of her insistent pleading. He explains to them that his mission is only to "the lost sheep of the house of Israel" (v. 24).

The woman comes to the Lord, worships him, and says, "Lord, help me" (v. 25). Further testing her faith, he says it is not proper "to take the children's bread, and cast it to dogs." It is not right to take that which was provided for the Jews, God's covenant people, and give it to Gentiles, who were not God's people and who worshiped false gods (v. 26). She agrees that this is so, but maintains that the dogs are allowed to eat "the crumbs that fall from their masters' table." In other words, if the Jews are not claiming all the grace of God, why should outsiders not receive a little of the unused portion (v. 27)?

Having drawn out and then displayed the woman's great faith, the Lord commends her highly and cures her daughter completely and instantaneously (v. 28).

JESUS HEALS MANY AND FEEDS FOUR THOUSAND (15:29-39)

After this Jesus returns to the neighborhood of the Sea of Galilee. Great crowds come up a mountainside to him, bringing their sick along. When Jesus heals them—the lame, the blind, the dumb, the maimed, and many others—they glorify the God of Israel. Evidently, many of the common people believe that Jesus is a man of God, even though many of them may not yet recognize him as God in human flesh (vv. 29-31).

Jesus performs another miracle that benefits a great company of people. He tells his disciples that the people have been with him for three days with nothing to eat. Furthermore, he will not dismiss them without food, lest they faint as they go (v. 32). His disciples, evidently forgetting the miraculous feeding of the five thousand not long before, ask him where they are to get enough bread to fill so great a multitude (v. 33). When Jesus asks how many loaves they have on hand, they answer, "Seven, and a few little fishes" (v. 34). Directing the multitude to be seated on the ground, Jesus takes the seven loaves and the fishes, gives thanks, divides, and hands the portions to his disciples, who in turn pass the food to the people (vv. 35–36). The Lord does not discard what they have, but uses it, although of course he could have created food from nothing had he chosen to do so. All the people, over four thousand, eat and are filled. And seven baskets full of fragments are gathered up afterward (vv. 37–38). The miracle occurred, presumably, in the disciples' act of distribution to the people.

The miracle of providing spiritual life and sustenance through the Word of God is worked by the Holy Spirit as we give the Word to others.

Following this, Jesus dismisses the people and passes over to Magdala by ship.

9

The King Promises to Build His Church

16:1–18:35

THE KING WARNS OF THE PHARISEES AND SADDUCEES (16:1–12)

1. **The King's rebuke of his enemies for their hypocritical request for "a sign from heaven" (vv. 1–4)**

   As chapter 16 opens, the Pharisees and Sadducees—temporarily working together, it would seem, against the

Lord Jesus—hypocritically ask Jesus to show them "a sign from heaven" (v. 1).

He answers sarcastically: They can tell from the sky what kind of weather is coming but seem to be unable to read "the signs of the times" (vv. 2–3).

Then he repeats what he had said earlier (12:39), that a wicked generation seeks a sign, but that no sign would be given it—that is, no further sign beyond the abundant signs or credentials already presented—except the sign of the prophet Jonah, which would be Christ's own resurrection.

So he leaves them and goes his way, crossing with his disciples to the other side of the Sea of Galilee. But the disciples forget to take bread along (vv. 4–5).

2. The Lord's warning to his disciples concerning the teaching of the Pharisees and Sadducees (vv. 5–12)

When Jesus warns them to beware of the leaven of the Pharisees and of the Sadducees, they think he is referring to the fact of their having forgotten to take bread (vv. 6–7).

Asking if they have forgotten his miraculous feeding of the five thousand and the four thousand, he tells them he was not referring to bread (vv. 8–11).

Then they understand that his warning about leaven referred to the teaching of the Pharisees and Sadducees (v. 12).

In other words, he is applying the parable of the leaven (13:33) and warns them to be on their guard lest they be influenced by the teachings of the Pharisees and Sadducees and doubt that he is the Messiah.

THE IDENTITY AND WORK OF THE KING
(16:13–20)

1. The identity of the King—"the Christ, the Son of the living God" (vv. 13–16)

A little later, apparently, the Lord asks his disciples an important question. Referring to himself as the Son of Man, he asks them what the people's opinion is regarding his identity (v. 13). They reply that there are various opinions—that he is John the Baptist or Elijah or Jeremiah, or one of the other prophets. Apparently many Jews in those days believed in reincarnation (v. 14). Then the Lord asks a much more personal question: What is your own opinion? Simon Peter answers, speaking, it would seem, for them all, and gives that clear, ringing testimony that has come down to us across the centuries: "You are the Christ, the Son of the living God."

2. Peter's confession—a revelation from the heavenly Father (v. 17)

Peter had stated the sublime fact of the Lord's Messiahship, not because some human being had told him, but because the Father in heaven had revealed it to him. Evidently the great difference between Peter and the Pharisees and Sadducees was this: Peter had faith to believe God, so God revealed the truth about his son to him; the Pharisees and Sadducees, though they too had heard his words, observed his life, and seen his miracles, had only hypocrisy and unbelief. Hence, God did not reveal his truth to them. See Matthew 11:25–27 and 13:9–17.

3. The Lord's prophecy concerning his Church (vv. 18-19)

a. Christ—the Foundation Stone of the Church (v. 18a)

Jesus further reveals truth to Peter, and in so doing makes a play on the Greek words translated "Peter" and "rock." The meaning seems to be as follows. Peter (Petros) is the kind of rock—a boulder or movable rock—which, while possessing certain elements of strength and stability, would be entirely unsuitable as a foundation for a building. But Jesus is going to build his church on the kind of rock (petra)—an immovable, solid rock or ledge—suitable for such a foundation. He is going to build his church—note the future tense—on himself, as the Christ, the Son of the living God. This accords with many other passages of Scripture. See, for example, Psalm 118:22-23; 1 Corinthians 3:10-11; Ephesians 2:19-21 and 1 Peter 2:5-7.

When Jesus says, "I will build my church," he indicates not only that such building is future ("I will"), but also who is to do the building ("I will"). He may and does use us, but it is he who does the building. Again, note whose Church it is to be ("my church"). It is to belong to no person, group, class, or organization but to him who purchased it with his own blood (Acts 20:28) and is building it.

b. A victorious church (v. 18b)

Jesus has more to say to Peter, and to us, regarding his church: "The gates of Hades shall not overpower it" (v. 18 NASB). This seems to guarantee not merely defensive victory for the church against the assaults of the power of Satan, symbolized by "the gates of Hades," but offensive victory as well. That is to say, the gates of Hades will not be strong enough to withstand the assaults of the church upon them. This is because he who is the head of the church is stronger than he who is the master of Hades gates. Millions upon millions of souls, imprisoned and held within the dark realm of sin and death over which Satan presides, have been liberated by the Lord Jesus Christ as he works through the agency of his church.

c. *The announcement concerning "the keys of the kingdom of heaven" and "the binding and loosing" (v. 19)*

The Lord Jesus has still more to say, not about the church, but about the kingdom of heaven. Addressing Peter personally, he says, "I will give unto *you* the keys of the kingdom of heaven: and whatever you bind on earth shall be bound in heaven: and whatever you loose on earth shall be loosed in heaven."

4. The basic difference between the church and the kingdom of heaven

Before discussing verse 19, let's consider the basic difference between the church and the kingdom of heaven. The church, as the word is used here and in many places in the epistles, consists of all true Christian believers during this dispensation—that is, from the Day of Pentecost, when the church on earth began, to the coming again of the Lord Jesus Christ, when the church will finish its earthly pilgrimage and be caught up to meet the Lord in the air. See Ephesians 1:22–23 and 1 Corinthians 12:12–14, 27; also Acts 2:1–4 and 1 Thessalonians 4:13–17. The kingdom of heaven, on the contrary, as used in Matthew

16 and in many other places, refers to all who *profess* to belong to the Lord Jesus, regardless of whether or not they have actually been born again. Thus the kingdom of heaven includes the church during this dispensation of grace and extends far beyond it. The church is the realm or sphere of *reality*; the kingdom of heaven, the realm or sphere of *profession*, which includes those who are genuine Christians and those who falsely claim to be Christians.

5. The explanation of verse 19

Note that the Lord promises to give Peter "the keys of the kingdom of heaven." Since the Bible is by far the best commentary on itself, we can look elsewhere in Scripture for references concerning Peter's acting in an official capacity. We have two such occurrences in Acts: one in chapter 2, where Peter preaches to Israel and uses the first "key" when he opens the sphere of Christian profession to the Jews at Pentecost; the other in chapter 10, where he preaches to Gentiles and uses the second "key" to open that same sphere of Christian profession to the rest of humanity. With respect to the rest of verse 19, the tense of the two Greek verbs, represented by "shall be bound" and "shall be loosed," indicates that the action in heaven *precedes* that on earth, and that Peter is merely carrying out decisions already reached in heaven.

The same words appear in Matthew 18:18 in connection with the Lord's teaching concerning church discipline (18:15–20). Without doubt, these two passages refer to this one subject. Revelation 1:18 proves that they have no reference to the salvation of souls, for the Lord Jesus himself holds "the keys of death and of Hades."

6. The Lord's charge to his disciples not to proclaim his Messiahship at that time (v. 20)

Having finished addressing Peter individually, the Lord instructs all his disciples to tell no one that he is the Christ. There were probably several reasons for this. First, it might start trouble with the leaders of Israel and the representatives of Rome. Second, the common people might make a further attempt to make him king on a purely material basis. Third, the fact he was indeed the Messiah of Old Testament prophecy was to be discerned on the basis of his life, his teachings, and his credentials rather than on what claims his disciples might make about him. All of this, of course, would change when he himself was no longer in the world. Then all would depend on what his followers would say about him and on the working of the Holy Spirit through them.

THE KING PREDICTS HIS SUFFERING, DEATH, AND GLORY (16:21–28)

1. Jesus' prediction of his death and resurrection (v. 21)

The remainder of chapter 16 is devoted to a series of predictions the Lord Jesus makes to his disciples. The first concerns himself. He must go—the "must" of his earthly mission—to Jerusalem, there to suffer, be killed, and rise the third day. Note that there is no "if" here.

2. Peter's rebuke and the Lord's answer (vv. 22–23)

Peter rebukes his Lord, urging him not to go to Jerusalem and die. Jesus then rebukes Peter as decidedly as he had commended him shortly before (see v. 17). Instead of being a mouthpiece for God, Peter is now a mouthpiece for Satan.

3. The cost and the reward of discipleship (vv. 24-27)

The second prediction is conditional. "If any man . . ." Jesus says. Just as he himself must suffer and die and rise and then be glorified, he calls on his disciples to do the same and receive an appropriate reward. In his own case, observe: "suffer," "be killed," "be raised again" (v. 21), and "the Son of man shall come in the glory of his Father" (v. 27); and in our case, observe: "deny himself," "take up his cross," "follow me" (v. 24), "lose his life for my sake," "find it" (v. 25), and "reward every man according to his works" (v. 27).

4. Jesus' prophecy of his transfiguration (v. 28)

The third prediction is absolute. There is no "if." Jesus says: "There be some standing here that shall not taste of death till they see the Son of man coming in his kingdom." Thus he foretells his own transfiguration, which is to be, for three of his disciples, a preview of his coming again in glory to set up his Kingdom on earth.

THE KING IS TRANSFIGURED (17:14-21)

1. The transfiguration (vv. 1-8)

Six days later Jesus takes Peter, James, and John up into a high mountain, where they see him transfigured. His face and raiment shine, and Moses and Elijah appear and talk with him (vv. 1-3). Luke tells us they were discussing his departure (i.e., from this life) at Jerusalem. Peter makes one of his famous blunders here, suggesting that they build three tabernacles, one for the Lord first. But the voice of God is heard from heaven saying: "This is my beloved son, in whom I am well pleased; hear him." In other words, the time has come to forget the Law and the prophets and to listen to the voice of the son of God, the beloved of his Father and the one in whom his Father takes perfect delight (vv. 4–5). The disciples are overcome with fear, but Jesus reassures them. When they look up, they see "no man, save Jesus only," which is just what the Father intended (vv. 6–8).

2. **The prophecy concerning Elijah and John the Baptist (vv. 9–13)**

When Jesus instructs Peter, James, and John to tell the vision to no one until after his resurrection, they ask why the scribes assert that Elijah must come before his own second advent. This is in accordance with Malachi 4:5–6. However, as to his first coming, Elijah—that is, John the Baptist, who came "in the spirit and power of Elijah"—had already come; and as they had mistreated John, so they would mistreat him (vv. 11–13). See Luke 1:13–17 and Matthew 11:12–14.

THE KING CURES A DEMONIAC, EPILEPTIC BOY (17:14–21)

While Jesus, Peter, James, and John were on the Mount of Transfiguration, the multitude below sees a heartrending spectacle. A man brings his epileptic, demon-possessed son to the rest of the disciples and they are unable to cure him.

The man appeals to Jesus (vv. 14–16) and, after characterizing that generation as "faithless and perverse," the Lord casts the demon out of the boy (vv. 17–18). When his disciples ask him why they were unable to cast him out, Jesus replies: "Because of your unbelief." He then says that faith makes the difference between impotence and power. In other words, through faith we can bring the power of God into any situation. Then he adds, "Nothing shall be impossible unto you" (vv. 19–21). This is true because "with God all things are possible" (Matt. 19:26).

Verse 21 does not appear in the American Standard Version.

THE KING AGAIN FORETELLS HIS DEATH AND RESURRECTION (17:22–23)

While still in Galilee, Jesus tells his disciples, for the second time, about his approaching death and resurrection. He says he will be betrayed "into the hands of men," put to death at their hands, and rise from the dead on the third day. Note the difference between this passage and Matthew 16:21–23. This time the disciples were "exceeding sorry," but there is no suggestion of interference.

THE KING AND THE HALF-SHEKEL TAX (17:24–27)

1. The necessity for humility (vv. 1–10)

The disciples ask the Lord: "Who is the greatest in the kingdom of heaven?" (v. 1).

The Lord uses this as an opportunity to teach a lesson in humility. Setting a little child in the midst of the disciples, he says that they must be converted and become as little children to enter the Kingdom, and that the most humble should be the greatest (vv. 2–4).

Evidently this conflicts with their thinking. Jesus goes on to show how important it is to have a right attitude of mind and heart. Receiving one such child in his name is equivalent to receiving him (v. 5), but causing a little one who believes in him to stumble is worthy of a dire penalty (v. 6).

Then, in words that remind us of Matthew 5:29–30, he warns of the terrible danger and awful consequences of failing to remove stumbling blocks from our lives (vv. 7–9). Solemnly, then, he warns his disciples not to despise one of these little ones whose angels are constantly beholding the face of his Father in heaven (v. 10).

2. The Savior's humility—the lost sheep—his will for "these little ones" (vv. 11-14)

Jesus seems to change the subject, but actually he is still on the same theme, as verse 14 shows. "The Son of man is come to save that which was lost" (v. 11).

Having made this wonderful statement regarding the purpose of his coming from heaven to earth, he gives a shortened version of the parable of the lost sheep (vv. 12–13). See Luke 15:3–7.

Then he assures them that their heavenly Father did not want any of these little ones to be lost (v. 14). Thus he teaches his disciples the value of humility. Those who are genuinely humble, like the publican in Luke 18:9–14, are the kind of people God wants to save and will save. Those who refuse to humble themselves before God will fail to receive his salvation.

THE KING GIVES LESSONS ON FORGIVENESS (18:15–35)

Having shown that God's forgiveness depends on genuine humility—without which there can be no real repentance for sin and faith in Christ for salvation—the Lord proceeds to show what God's forgiveness should accomplish *in* us. The instruction is in two parts, the first having to do with the genuineness of forgiveness.

1. **The proper way to deal with a sinning brother (vv. 15–20)**

If one believer sins against another, the aggrieved one should go to the other alone and attempt to straighten the matter out privately (v. 15). If the person will not listen, the believer is to take one or two others along and visit the person again. Thus, if it becomes necessary to take the matter to others, there will be two or three witnesses as to what was said (v. 16). If the offender still refuses to listen, the matter is to be taken to the local church. If the person neglects to hear the church, he or she is to be treated by the aggrieved person as an outsider (v. 17).

Three very important pronouncements by the Lord follow. First, there is to be correspondence between action on earth and in heaven. Here, as in Matthew 16:19, the tense of the verbs in the Greek indicates that the action in heaven precedes that on earth. The church is to carry out on earth the decisions already made in heaven (v. 18). What a heavy responsibility this places on the Church: to discern and carry out the mind of God! Second, there is the assurance that if two believers agree on earth regarding anything, that thing will be done by the Father in heaven (v. 19). This seems, in view of verse 18, to mean that if two believers receive the assurance that the Father wants such a thing done, and pray accordingly, the Father will do it. Third, there is the assurance that where two or three are gathered together in the name of the Lord Jesus Christ, he is in their midst (v. 20). This seems to indicate that his presence depends on the genuineness of their being assembled in his name—honestly seeking his will, and honestly attempting to act for him—and that under such conditions he will reveal his will and guide them in their action.

2. The genuineness of forgiveness (vv. 21–35)

Jesus takes the occasion afforded by Peter's question to go into this matter in some detail. Jesus tells Peter he is to forgive a brother who sins against him not merely seven times, but seventy times seven times—that is, indefinitely (vv. 21–22). To explain further, he tells a parable of the kingdom of heaven.

One of the servants of a certain king owed his master a huge sum (vv. 23–24). Having nothing with which to pay, the king gave orders that all the man's possessions, including wife and children, were to be sold for the debt. The man pleaded for mercy, and the king compassionately forgave him his debt (vv. 25–27). Thereupon that servant looked up a fellow servant who owed him a trifling sum and violently demanded payment. When the fellow servant pleaded for mercy, he refused and had him thrown into prison (vv. 28–30). When the king heard about this, he sent for the first servant and said to him: "You wicked servant, I forgave you all that debt because you desired me: should not you also have had compassion on your fellow servant, even as I had pity on you?" (vv.

31–33). Then his lord delivered him to the tormentors until all the huge debt was paid (v. 34).

Jesus then applies the parable: "So likewise shall my heavenly Father do unto you, if you from your hearts do not forgive every brother who trespasses" (v. 35).

This wicked servant does not represent genuine, believing Christians who are not as generous as they might be, but professing Christians who never really repented of their sins and trusted Christ as Savior. There was no genuine humility. His "forgiveness" was potential, not actual, or else his lord could not have demanded payment later. Further, his lord characterizes him as "wicked," and the Lord Jesus in his comment says, "My heavenly Father," indicating mere profession. "Your heavenly Father" would have indicated new birth.

10

The King Enters Jerusalem

19:1–21:46

THE SANCTITY OF MARRIAGE (19:1–12)

1. **Jesus in the borders of Judea, healing the multitudes (vv. 1–2)**

   Following the events of the last chapter, our Lord leaves Galilee and goes into the borders of Judea on the east of Jordan. Great crowds follow him, and he heals them.

2. The Lord's answer to the hypocritical question of the Pharisees about divorce (vv. 3–6)

The Pharisees come with a question about divorce: "Is it lawful for a man to put away his wife for every cause?" Jesus refers them to what God said at the very beginning (see Gen. 1:27; 2:24), namely, that he had created them male and female and that, therefore, "the two shall be one flesh." Then Jesus adds this comment: "What God has joined together, let not man separate."

3. His further teaching about marriage and divorce (vv. 7–9)

When the Pharisees object that Moses made provision for divorce (Deut. 24:1–4), Jesus explains that Moses permitted divorce under certain circumstances because of the people's sinfulness, but that "from the beginning it was not so." In other words, under the Law of Moses, divorce was permitted in certain instances but it was never God's intention for his people and it was permitted only to avoid some greater evil.

Jesus adds the principle which, it seems, should guide Christians today, stating that fornication is grounds for divorce and remarriage. Divorce and remarriage under any other circumstances are the same as adultery, as is marrying someone who has been divorced for any other reason.

4. His answer to the disciples' question about marriage (vv. 10–12)

When his disciples remark that it is wise, then, not to marry at all, Jesus explains that it is better for some not to marry. Some are sterile from birth; some have been sterilized; and some have sterilized themselves for the sake of the kingdom of heaven. It is quite possible, if not probable, that the last statement is to be understood figuratively—that is, that there are some who have been willing to forego marriage for the sake of the kingdom.

ENTRANCE INTO THE KINGDOM (19:13-26)

1. "Of such is the kingdom of heaven" (vv. 13-15)

In this section, our Lord uses two incidents to teach basic lessons about entrance into the kingdom of heaven. The first concerns some little children who were brought to Jesus for his blessing. The disciples object to this, presumably thinking it an unreasonable burden to put on the Lord. But Jesus says to let the little ones come to him, and then adds this significant statement: "For of such is the kingdom of heaven." This is in perfect harmony with his teaching in chapter 18. Genuine humility is required to enter the kingdom. Evidently, our Lord is not referring to mere profession of faith, but to the reality of it. He lays his hands on the children; then he goes elsewhere.

2. The rich young ruler (vv. 16-26)

The second incident in this section concerns a rich young man, described in Luke 18:18 as a ruler. Note the question the rich man asks: "Good Master, what good thing shall I do, that I may have eternal life?" (v. 16). Jesus answers first with a question: "Why do you call me good?" Then he continues, "There is none good but one, that is, God: but if you will enter into life, keep the commandments" (v. 17).

There are two important points here. First, Jesus is asking the man if he really means what is implied in the salutation, "Good Master." If he does, he is acknowledging that Jesus is God. Second, Jesus answers in a way that shows it is impossible to "enter into life" by doing, since doing requires one to "keep the commandments"—something no one but Christ has ever done or can do. Jesus wants to show the man how hopeless a task this is, so that he will stop trying to earn eternal life and will trust Christ for it instead. But instead the man asks, "Which ones?" Jesus lists eight of them, and still the man does not get the point Jesus is trying to make. He self-righteously claims that he has kept all these from his youth up (v. 20). The Lord Jesus wisely tells him to prove that claim by selling all his possessions and giving the proceeds to the poor, and then to come and follow him. But the young man is not able or willing to obey and goes "away sorrowful" (vv. 21–22).

Jesus uses this incident to show his disciples how difficult it is for a rich person to enter into the kingdom (v. 23). Then he explains to his astonished disciples that "it is easier for a camel to go through the eye of a needle, than for a rich man to enter into the kingdom of God." That is, it is utterly impossible for a rich person—or a poor one either for that matter—to be saved through his or her own efforts. But God can save, for "with God all things are possible" (vv. 24–26).

POSITION IN THE KINGDOM (19:27–30)

After hearing the conversation between Jesus and the rich young ruler, Peter raises a question: "We have forsaken all, and followed you; what shall we have therefore?" (v. 27). Jesus' reply may be divided into two parts. The first is a direct reply to Peter's question and refers only to the Twelve. They are to sit on twelve thrones, judging the twelve tribes of Israel, when Israel as a nation is "born again" and "the son of man shall sit in the throne of his glory"—that is, in the Millennium, (v. 28). The second part of his answer concerns all who have made sacrifices for Christ's name's sake. They will receive a bountiful reward and "inherit everlasting life." However, many who are first now will be last in the end, and many who are last now will be first then (vv. 29–30).

LABORERS IN THE VINEYARD (20:1-16)

1. The parable (vv. 1-15; cf. 19:30 with 20:16)

Actually, there is no break here. The Lord goes right on with the parable of the laborers in the vineyard to explain his statement about the first who will be last and the last who will be first. The kingdom of heaven is like a situation in which a householder hires laborers at various times throughout the day to work in his vineyard. He agrees to pay the first group "a penny a day" (vv. 1–2). He hires four other groups during the day, assuring each that he will give them "whatsoever is right" (vv. 3–7). At the end of the day, he instructs his steward to pay the laborers, beginning with the last group hired and working back to the first. When the last group were given a penny each, those who had worked all day expected to be given more but were disappointed (vv. 8–10). When they complained, the householder explained that he had given them exactly what had been agreed upon (vv. 11–13). But he does not stop there. He goes on to say that he has a right to do as he chooses with what is his, and he chooses to give those who had worked only a part of the day the same amount he had agreed to give those who worked the whole day. Then he rebukes the man with the question: "Is your eye evil because I am good?" We might put it this way: "Are you covetous because I am generous?" Then Jesus repeats the statement about the last who shall be first, and the first last (vv. 14–16).

2. The reward for service according to faithfulness to opportunity

This parable illustrates the truth that God will always do right. He will keep every promise. But he will also be gracious and do more than he has promised, if he chooses, and will reward every servant of his not only according to the amount of service rendered, but also according to the spirit in which it was rendered. Since all the laborers were working for the same householder, we can conclude that they represent saints working for rewards, not sinners working for salvation.

THE KING AGAIN FORETELLS HIS PASSION (20:17–19)

Jesus is on his way to Jerusalem for his last visit before his crucifixion. He takes his disciples aside and for the third time at least (see also Matt. 16:21; 17:22–23) foretells his death and resurrection. This time he goes into great detail, mentioning no less than ten items connected with those vitally important facts. First, he will be betrayed. Second, his betrayal will be to the chief priests and scribes. Third, they will condemn him. Fourth, their condemnation will be to death. Fifth, they will deliver him to the Gentiles. Sixth, the Gentiles will mock him. Seventh, they will scourge him. Eighth, they will crucify him. Ninth, he will rise again. And tenth, his resurrection will be on the third day. Every detail was literally fulfilled.

THE KING TEACHES HUMILITY AND HEALS TWO BLIND MEN (20:20–34)

1. The ambitious request of James, John, and their mother; the Lord's answer (vv. 20–23)

The Lord's teaching on humility grows out of the ambition of two of his twelve disciples and their mother. The mother of Zebedee's children comes to Jesus with her two sons (James and John), and requests that they be given the places of chief honor in his kingdom—one on his right, the other on his left (vv. 20–21). Although the mother makes the request, the sons are guilty too, and the Lord addresses them in his reply: "You do not know what you ask." Then he asks them if they are able to drink of the cup he is to drink and to receive the baptism he is to receive. They egotistically respond, "We are able" (v. 22). The Lord assures them that they will indeed drink of his cup and receive the baptism he is to receive, referring probably to their persecution and suffering on his behalf (see Acts 12:1–2; Rev. 1:9). He says, however, that it is not his to give the privilege of sitting on his right and on his left, but his Father's (v. 23).

2. Humble service—the way to greatness (vv. 24–28)

When the other ten disciples hear about this request, they are indignant at James and John, possibly provoked that they had not thought of it first (v. 24). So Jesus calls them all and explains that humility is to be the rule among them, and that the way to greatness is to serve the rest, and the way to be greatest is to be a bond servant or slave to the rest. To impress this truth on them and to direct their minds to the basic reason for his incarnation, he cites his own example in coming from heaven to earth "not to be ministered unto, but to minister, and to give his life a ransom for many" (vv. 25–28).

These thrilling words from the lips of our Lord leave no excuse for anyone who can read the Word of God to be ignorant of the fundamental reason for his first advent.

3. Jesus' healing of two blind men (vv. 29–34)

As the Lord and his disciples continue on their way to Jerusalem, they pass through Jericho. As they are leaving the city, a great multitude follows Jesus. As they move along the road, two blind men cry out to him: "Have mercy on us, O Lord, son of David" (vv. 29–30). The crowd tries to hush them up, but they cry out all the more, until Jesus stands still and calls them to him, asking what they want. They reply that they want him to give them sight. The Lord, moved with compassion, touches their eyes. The men receive sight and follow him (vv. 31–34).

How often since then, in response to the cry of faith, has the Lord done the same thing in the spiritual realm!

THE KING RIDES INTO THE CITY (21:1–17)

1. The official presentation of the King to the nation of Israel (vv. 1–11)

Approaching Jerusalem, they reach the Mount of Olives, just east of the city. Jesus sends two of his disciples into the nearby village of Bethphage to loose a certain ass and her colt and to bring them to him. To anyone who asks what they are doing, Jesus tells the disciples to reply, "The Lord needs them" (vv. 1–3). This, says Matthew, was done in fulfillment of Zechariah's prophecy (9:9) which he quotes: "Tell the daughter of Sion, Behold, your King comes unto you, meek, sitting upon an ass, and a colt the foal of an ass" (vv. 4–5). The original prophecy also contains explanatory words not quoted by Matthew: "He is just, and having salvation."

When the two disciples return with the animals, they put their garments on them and the Lord Jesus sits thereon. A vast number of Jews are in Jerusalem at this time for the celebration of the Passover, and a great multitude spread their garments in the road and strewed the way with branches of trees. The multitudes before and behind unite in their acclaim, saying: "Hosanna to the son of David: Blessed is he who comes in the name of the Lord; Hosanna in the highest" (vv. 6–9). "Hosanna" means "save now." The bulk of the acclamation is taken from Psalm 118:25–26. Presumably those who thus acclaimed the Lord were disciples of his from all over the Holy Land, for in Luke 19:37 they are described as "the whole multitude of the disciples."

The whole of Jerusalem is stirred by the reception accorded him; and when the question is asked, "Who is this?" the multitude responds: "This is Jesus the prophet of Nazareth of Galilee" (vv. 10–11). This response indicates that, while they acclaimed him as a prophet, most of them did not realize that he was "the Christ, the Son of the living God."

2. The Lord's second cleansing of the Temple (vv. 12–14)

Upon entering the city, Jesus goes into the Temple. There he finds people buying and selling and changing money, and he drives them out, saying: "It is written [see Isa.

56:7], My house shall be called the house of prayer; but you have made it a den of thieves" (vv. 12–13; see Jer. 7:11). Evidently they had been cheating the people. This is the second clearing, or cleansing, of the Temple by our Lord. The first, two or three years earlier, is recorded in John 2:13–17. After this, the blind and lame come to him in the Temple, and he heals them (v. 14).

3. Jesus accepts worship—a further claim to Messiahship (vv. 15–17)

Following these things, the children in the Temple cry out in his praise, "Hosanna to the son of David." But the chief priests and scribes, greatly displeased, come to him and ask if he hears what they are saying. He replies: "Have you never read, Out of the mouth of babes and sucklings you have perfected praise?" See Psalm 8:2. The Lord is implying that hypocrisy may come from the lips of adults but truth may be heard from the lips of little children. Thus he approves what the children are saying; that is, he affirms that he is indeed the Messiah, the Son of David, and is also the One who can save. Saying this, he leaves them and goes out to Bethany, a suburb, for the night.

THE KING AGAIN REBUKES UNBELIEF (21:18–27)

1. The cursing of the barren fig tree (vv. 18–22)

Jesus returns to Jerusalem from Bethany the next morning—probably Monday—he sees a fig tree bearing leaves but no fruit. He is hungry, and finding no fruit on the tree he curses it and it withers away, to the astonishment of the disciples (vv. 18–20). This symbolizes the setting aside of Israel because of their lack of faith and fruit.

Then Jesus speaks of the power of faith, telling his disciples that if they pray, believing, greater miracles than the withering of the fig tree will be accomplished, even the seemingly impossible. Israel produced no fruit for the glory of God—the reason, unbelief. But they, the disciples, have the privilege of producing great fruit for the glory of God if only they will believe him (vv. 21–22). The principle is simple: faith, fruit; no faith, no fruit.

2. The question of the authority of Christ (vv. 23–27)

Going into the Temple again and teaching, Jesus is approached by the chief priests and elders who ask, "By what authority do you do these things?" and "Who gave you this authority?" Jesus, perceiving their hypocrisy, asks them a question, promising to answer theirs if they will answer his (vv. 23–24). He asks, "The baptism of John . . . was it from heaven or from men?" This puts them in a dilemma. If they say, "From heaven," Jesus will immediately ask them the unanswerable question, "Then why didn't you believe him?" But if they say, "Of men," the people, who considered John a prophet, will turn on them. So they try to evade the question, saying, "We cannot tell." Jesus replies that he, then, will not tell them by what authority he is acting. He exposes them as hypocrites and then refuses to tell them something that should already be perfectly evident to them, and would have been had they been sincere in asking. Again their lack of faith is shown, and with it their hypocritical hearts (vv. 25–27).

MORE PARABLES OF THE KINGDOM (21:28-46)

Following his answer to their hypocritical question, Jesus tells the chief priests and elders two parables designed to show them that he knows the wickedness of their hearts.

1. The parable of a man and his two sons (vv. 28-32)

To his first son a man said, "Son, go work today in my vineyard." The son curtly replied, "I will not." Afterward, however, he changed his mind and went (vv. 28-29).

To the second son, the father spoke similarly. This son politely answered, "I go, sir." But he did not go (v. 30).

Jesus asks, "Which of the two did his father's will?" They correctly reply, "The first." Then Jesus applies the parable to the chief priests and elders, assuring them that the publicans and harlots who believe the preaching of John will go into the kingdom of God before they do (v. 31).

2. The parable of the householder and his vineyard (vv. 33-41)

A householder planted a vineyard and provided everything necessary to maintain it. Then he put the vineyard in the care of husbandmen and left for a distant land (v. 33). As harvest time approached, he sent his servants to get fruit from the husbandmen. But instead of fruit, they gave them ill-treatment and death. Similar treatment was accorded other servants he sent to them (vv. 34-36). As a last resort, he sent his son to them, saying, "They will respect my son." But instead they killed the son, intending to seize the vineyard for themselves (vv. 37-39).

The Lord asks the chief priests and elders a question: "When the Lord of the vineyard comes, what will he do to those husbandmen?" Again they answer correctly, saying: "He will miserably destroy those wicked men and will let out his vineyard to other husbandmen, who will give him the fruits in their seasons" (vv. 40–41).

3. The Lord's application of the parable—another claim to Messiahship (vv. 42–44)

Taking the words from their mouths, the Lord applies this parable also to them. In fulfillment of the prophecy of Psalm 118:22–23, he says, "The stone which the builders rejected, the same is become the head of the corner." He himself is the Son, the Heir, and the Stone. Rejected by the leaders of Israel, and murdered, he is to become the Cornerstone upon which the whole building of God is to rest (v. 42).

In 1 Peter 2:3–8 we read that this is precisely what has taken place. "Therefore," says Jesus, "the kingdom of God shall be taken from you, and given to a nation bringing forth the fruits thereof" (v. 43).

That is, the true kingdom is to be taken away from the Jews, as a nation, and given to the Gentiles, who will produce fruit for God.

This has been true now for some nineteen hundred years. The great majority of Christians have been Gentiles, not Jews.

To fall on Christ, the Stone, is to be broken in humility and repentance for sin; but to have the Stone fall on us, is to be judged and crushed by Christ, the very one who could have been our Savior (v. 44).

4. The anger of the Pharisees and their fear of the people (vv. 45-46)

The chief priests and Pharisees—the latter probably are the "elders" mentioned in verse 23—perceive that these parables refer to them. Angered, they try to seize Jesus. However, for fear of the people who regard Jesus as a prophet, they decide to wait (vv. 45-46).

11

The King Teaches and Reproves

22:1–23:39

THE KING TELLS THE PARABLE OF THE MARRIAGE FEAST (22:1–14)

1. The parable

Jesus says the kingdom of heaven is like a situation in which a king makes a wedding feast (NASB) for his son (vv. 1–2). The invited guests refuse to come when summoned, giving a variety of foolish excuses (vv. 3–5). Some take the king's messengers and kill them (v. 6). The king, hearing of this, sends out his armies, destroys the murderers, and burns up their city (v. 7). Then the king instructs his servants to gather in guests, good and bad alike, from the highways. Many accept the invitation, and the wedding is furnished with guests (vv. 8–10). When the king comes in to see the guests, he sees a man without a wedding garment. When questioned, the man is speechless, having no excuse to offer. The custom was for the king to provide a wedding garment for each guest. This man evidently disdained the king's wedding garment, preferring his own (vv. 11–12). The king then directs his servants to bind the man and cast him into outer darkness. For, said Jesus, "Many are called, but few are chosen" (vv. 13–14).

2. The explanation of the parable

The symbolism in this parable appears to be as follows: The king is God the Father. The king's son is the Lord Jesus Christ. And the marriage feast celebrates the union of Christ and his elect. Israel was his elect, but they despised the call of God through his prophets and messengers. Accordingly, God judged them, chastising them severely and burning up their city, Jerusalem. (This occurred about forty years later, in A.D. 70.)

For about two thousand years the good and the bad of the whole world have been invited to the wedding feast of the king's son. Many have accepted, and ultimately the wedding will be filled with guests. However, the Church, not Israel, is the bride, made up of the good and the bad from among Jews and Gentiles who, all during this age of grace, accept God's loving invitation.

The man without a wedding garment represents those robed in their own self-righteousness instead of the righteousness provided by the crucified and risen Savior. See Isaiah 61:9–10 and 2 Corinthians 5:21.

THE KING ANSWERS THREE QUESTIONS (22:15-40)

1. Pharisees, Sadducees, Herodians

During the days of our Lord on earth, the bulk of the Jews—or at least their leaders—seem to have been divided into three groups: the Pharisees, the Sadducees, and the Herodians. The Pharisees were the *orthodox* religious party, strictly observing the letter of the Law of Moses but overlooking the spirit of it altogether. They are described in Matthew 15:8–9. The Sadducees were the *liberal* party, very religious but discarding the supernatural. They are described in Acts 23:8. The Herodians were a *political* party, composed of those who favored Herod and the Roman conquerors. On occasion, two of these groups would work together against our Lord—as indicated in Matthew 16:1, when Pharisees and Sadducees join forces; and here in Matthew 22:15–16, when Pharisees and Herodians try to entangle him in his teaching (vv. 15–16).

2. "Is it lawful to give tribute unto Caesar, or not?" (vv. 15-22)

They ask him a question that embraces both realms of politics and religion: "Is it lawful to give tribute unto Caesar, or not?" (v. 17). Undoubtedly what they meant was: Is it consistent with the Law of Moses to do so? Jesus, knowing their evil design, asks them to show him a piece of the tribute money. They show him a penny, or denarius (vv. 18–19 NASB). The Lord then asks whose image and superscription, or inscription, appear on it. They answer, "Caesar's." The Lord Jesus then gives his answer, which has come ringing down to us through the centuries: "Render therefore unto Caesar the things that are Caesar's; and unto God the things that are God's" (vv. 20–21).

Jesus' answer means, first, that they have already answered their own question. Their use of the tribute money is in itself an acknowledgment of Caesar, since his image and superscription are on it. Second, it means that while there are duties owed to Caesar, or government, it must never be forgotten that there are also duties owed to God.

Jesus' reply completely silenced them and sent them on their way (v. 22).

3. Is there a resurrection of the dead? (vv. 23–33)

Following this the Sadducees come with a question in the realm of religion or theology. With pretended piety they base their question on a provision in the Law of Moses. See Deuteronomy 25:5–6. The Sadducees make up a hypothetical case. They ask, if a woman marries and becomes a widow seven times, "In the resurrection, whose wife will she be of the seven? for they all had her." (vv. 23–28). They are trying to ridicule the doctrine of resurrection, making it appear inconsistent with the instruction of Moses. Evidently they are also trying to discredit the Lord's teaching of the doctrine of resurrection. This seems to have been an issue of particular interest at the time because shortly before this Jesus had said: "I am the resurrection, and the life . . ." (John 11:25–26); and had then proceeded to raise Lazarus from the grave.

The Lord Jesus answers the Sadducees by telling them they are in error, being ignorant of two things: the Scriptures and the power of God—the very things many professing Christians are ignorant of today. Then he demolishes their argument by stating that in the resurrection there is no such thing as marriage (vv. 29–30). Then he refers to God's words to Moses recorded in Exodus 3:6: "I am . . . the God of Abraham, the God of Isaac, and the God of Jacob." At that time Abraham, Isaac, and Jacob had all been dead for many years; yet God—who "is not the God of the dead, but of the living"— uses the present "I am" rather than "I was." Thus he proves both that life after death is a reality, and that Moses taught the doctrine of resurrection. The people, hearing these things, are astonished at his teaching (vv. 31–33).

4. "Which is the great commandment in the law?" (vv. 34–40)

The Sadducees, having been silenced by the Lord, and the Pharisees consult together. One of the latter asks the Lord Jesus a question—not honestly, for information, but hypocritically, as indicated by the phrase "tempting him" (vv. 34–35). The question is, "Which is the great commandment in the law?" (v. 36). The questioner thought he could put Jesus in an embarrassing position by making him label one commandment as more important or binding than the rest. However, he did not expect the answer Jesus gave. Jesus quotes Moses, whom this lawyer pretended to respect so highly. "You shall love the Lord your God with all your heart, and with all your soul, and with all your mind. This is the first and great commandment" (vv. 37–38). This is not only the truth, it is the truth from Moses himself, and is so evidently the truth that debate is ridiculous. Furthermore, it strongly hints at one of the glaring errors of the Pharisees, for it shows that duty to God is more important than duty to man.

Jesus elaborates, without being asked, and says that the second commandment is similar to the first: "You shall love your neighbor as yourself." He quotes this from Leviticus 19:18. "On these two commandments," says Jesus, "hang all the law and the prophets" (vv. 39–40). In other words, the whole Old Testament may be summed up in these two divine commands concerning love to God and man.

THE KING ASKS ONE QUESTION (22:41–46)

"What do you think of Christ? Whose son is he?"

Having silenced the Pharisees, Herodians, Sadducees, and now the Pharisees again, Jesus propounds a question to the last group. "What do you think of Christ? Whose son is he?" They answer him correctly: "The son of David" (vv. 41–42). That, however, is only part of the answer. So Jesus inquires further. If that is so, why does David refer to his son (or offspring) as his Lord, as he plainly does in Psalm 110:1? As Jesus indicates, a man does not normally refer to his own offspring as his Lord (vv. 43–45). His listeners were unwilling to give the obvious answer, that this Old Testament Scripture clearly indicated that the Christ, or Messiah, when he came, would be not only the Son of David, but also the Son of God.

After this no one dared ask him any more questions (v. 46).

THE KING EXHORTS TO HUMILITY (23:1–12)

Turning now from the Pharisees, the Lord addresses the multitude and his disciples. Using the scribes and Pharisees as an object lesson, he teaches them to be humble. He instructs them to do as these men say, but not as they do (vv. 1–3). Then he gets more specific. They have no real love or they would not require so much of people and then fail to help them in any way (v. 4). They have no real humility or they would not make themselves so prominent and revel in being greeted as "Rabbi" or "Teacher" (vv. 5–7). Do not be like them, he says, for Christ is your only "Master," or authoritative teacher, and you are all brethren, that is, you are all on an equal footing (vv. 8–10). This does not mean that no person is entitled to be regarded as a leader or teacher (that would contradict 1 Corinthians 12:28 and Ephesians 4:11–12, to say nothing of Hebrews 13:7, 17); but it does mean that Christ is the Lord of all of us and that we are all brothers and sisters in him and under him. Furthermore, Jesus says that the greatest among Christians shall serve, or minister to, the rest. Then he states a principle that is given repeatedly in Scripture: "Whoever exalts himself will be abased; and he who humbles himself will be exalted" (vv. 11–12). See Matthew 20:25–28; also Philippians 2:8–9; James 4:6; 1 Peter 5:5.

THE KING PRONOUNCES SEVEN WOES (23:13–36)

Apparently some of the Pharisees who had tried to ensnare the Lord Jesus are still standing by. Jesus turns to them and addresses them directly with a series of scathing denunciations. He exposes them as hypocrites and blind guides, insincere in themselves and leading others astray.

His first charge against them is that they refuse to enter the kingdom of heaven themselves and refuse to permit others to enter (v. 13).

His second charge is that they foreclose on widows' houses, while hypocritically making long prayers (v. 14). (This "woe" does not appear in some manuscripts.)

His third charge (vv. 15–22)—or, according to the American Standard Version, his second (v. 15) and third (beginning with v. 16)—covers two things: making proselytes and swearing by various things. Jesus accuses the scribes and Pharisees of going to extreme lengths to make Gentiles accept the Jewish faith. But when finished with them, Jesus says, they are "twofold more the child of hell than" themselves (v. 15). Furthermore, they teach that swearing by the Temple is not binding, but swearing by the gold of the Temple is! How foolish and deceitful, since it is the Temple that sanctifies or hallows the gold (v. 16–17)! Likewise with the altar and the gift laid on the altar(vv. 18–19). Furthermore, says Jesus, swearing by the altar involves everything on it; and to swear by the Temple means to swear by it and by him who dwells in it; and to swear by heaven means to swear by the throne of God and by God himself who sits upon the throne (vv. 20–22).

The fourth charge our Lord brings against the scribes and Pharisees deals with the observance of the Law of Moses. They pay tithes of the small and relatively unimportant garden herbs—mint, anise, and cummin—but omit the really important things, such as justice (NASB), mercy, and faith (vv. 23–24).

The fifth charge concerns their extreme care regarding the physical and ceremonial cleanliness of dishes and utensils but their utter disregard for honesty and self-control (vv. 25–26).

The sixth charge against them has to do with their pretended righteousness, when in reality they are full of hypocrisy and iniquity. The Lord Jesus likens them to whitewashed tombs, beautiful on the outside, but on the inside "full of dead men's bones and of all uncleanness" (vv. 27–28).

The seventh and last charge he levels against them has to do with their treatment of the prophets and other righteous men God had sent to them. They build the tombs and garnish or decorate the sepulchers of such men, who had been ill-treated and killed by their fathers; yet they themselves do and will do the same (vv. 29–34). Thus, says Jesus, upon them and their generation shall come the blood of righteous men from Abel to Zachariah (vv. 35–36). He is referring, undoubtedly, to John the Baptist, himself, Stephen, and others.

THE KING'S LAMENT OVER JERUSALEM
(23:37–39)

The Lord follows his denunciation of the scribes and Pharisees with a touching lament over Jerusalem. The city he would gladly have gathered to himself, for protection and fellowship, preferred to kill the prophets and stone the messengers of God. Therefore, he says, "Your house is left unto you desolate." He is leaving the Temple, not merely physically but spiritually as well; and they shall not see him again until he returns in glory and they receive him as the one who comes from God.

12

The King Foretells the Coming Kingdom

24:1–25:46

THE DESTRUCTION OF THE TEMPLE (24:1-2)

Jesus leaves the Temple for the last time before his crucifixion and his disciples call his attention to the work of construction apparently still going on at the Temple after more than forty-six years. See John 2:20. In response the Lord told them that one day the entire Temple would be leveled. This actually occurred when the Romans destroyed Jerusalem about forty years later, in A.D. 70.

THE PREACHING OF THE GOSPEL OF THE KINGDOM (24:3-14)

1. The disciples' three questions (v. 3)

His disciples come to him privately and ask him three questions:
- a. *When is the Temple to be destroyed?*
- b. *What is to be the sign of the Lord's Second Coming?*
- c. *What is to be the sign of the end of the age?*

The answer to the first question is not recorded in Matthew, but it is given in Luke 21:20-24 (note v. 24 particularly). The other two questions are answered in Matthew 24.

2. "The beginning of sorrows" (vv. 4-12)

A number of things are to take place before the Lord comes back to set up his kingdom at the end of this dispensation, or the age of grace. First, there will be false teaching and false Christs (vv. 4-5) followed by wars and other calamities (v. 8). These things have characterized the nineteen centuries and more that have followed the death and resurrection of Christ. But after these things, there will be persecution of the Lord's people for the sake of the name of Jesus (v. 9). Then will follow hatred, betrayal, false prophets, iniquity, and a waning devotion to the Lord (vv. 10-12).

3. Deliverance from the tribulation at the return of Christ in glory (v. 13)

"But he who endures to the end shall be saved." This, it seems, does not refer to eternal salvation but rather to deliverance, through the return of the Lord, from the terrible persecution of those days (see v. 22).

4. "The Gospel of the kingdom" (v. 14)

Observe the Lord's next word: "And this Gospel of the kingdom shall be preached in all the world for a witness unto all nations; and then shall the end come." The Gospel of the kingdom was preached by John the Baptist (see Matthew 3:1–2) and by Jesus (see Matthew 4:17). Being preached now, instead, is the Gospel of salvation from sin (see 1 Corinthians 15:1–4). But just before the Lord's return, the Gospel of the kingdom will again be preached by his people, believing Jews, in all the inhabited earth. "And then shall the end come"—the end of this age (see v. 3) and the Lord's return (see v. 27)

THE GREAT TRIBULATION (24:15-22)

The Lord continues to answer the disciples' questions and deals in particular with certain phases of the awful period of persecution of the Jews, variously known in Scripture as the "great tribulation" (v. 21 and Revelation 7:14); the "time of Jacob's trouble" (Jeremiah 30:7); and a "time of trouble" (Daniel 12:1). The signal that the great tribulation is about to break on the Jews in Palestine in those days will be the sight of the "abomination of desolation" standing in the Holy Place of their Temple (v. 15). This evidently is an abomination, or idol, that defiles the Temple and makes God-fearing Jews desert it. See Daniel

9:27; 11:31; 12:11; 2 Thessalonians 2:3–4; Revelation 13:14–15. Orthodox, Sabbath-keeping Jews will flee for their lives, for the time of their awful persecution will have come (vv. 16–21). For the sake of the elect, this period of time will be shortened, lest none survive.

THE SECOND COMING (24:23–31)

1. The Lord's warning against false Christs (vv. 23–25)

The great tribulation of Israel is to be immediately followed by the Lord's return. Furthermore, his return will be so public that no one will seek for him. There will be many false Christs and false prophets, some performing great signs and wonders to deceive even the elect, if possible. But the elect have been warned about this in advance.

2. The return of Christ—a visible, glorious appearing (vv. 26–28)

The coming of the true Christ will be as public as the lightning that flashes from the eastern sky to the western (vv. 26–27). Verse 28 may be explained by Revelation 19:17–18.

3. The events at Christ's return (vv. 29–31)

Sun, moon, and stars will be greatly affected immediately following the great tribulation. Some think this symbolizes great political and governmental upheavals. Then the sign of the Son of Man will appear in heaven, followed by the public appearance of the Son of Man himself "coming in the clouds of heaven with power and great glory." What a day! All the tribes of earth will mourn because they evidently realize that the one they previously rejected is to be their Judge (vv. 29–30).

Then he will gather his elect together from the four quarters of the earth (v. 31). This, presumably, is so they may go into the kingdom (see Matthew 25:34).

SIGNS OF THE SECOND COMING (24:32–51)

Turning from the program of the Second Coming, the Lord indicates the signs of his coming.

1. The sign of the fig tree (vv. 32–35)

Just as they knew summer was approaching by the appearance of leaves on the fig trees, so people would know Christ's coming was near by the evidences of spiritual life in Israel and the events spoken of earlier in the chapter. The fig tree, like the vine, is used in Scripture as a symbol of Israel (see 1 Kings 4:25; Micah 4:4; Habakkuk 3:17; Matthew 21:19).

Then the Lord makes a profound statement that has held true for more than nineteen hundred years. Israel will survive dispersion and persecution, tribulation and massacre, to our own day—and will until Christ returns (vv. 32–35). The story is told that Frederick the Great called for a Christian theologian to prove with one word the inspiration of the Bible. The theologian answered, "Jew."

2. The sign of the days of Noah—the element of complete surprise (vv. 36–41)

The second sign pertains to the days of Noah. Concerning the *time* of his return, the Lord Jesus said, "Of that day and hour no man knows, no, not the angels of heaven, but my Father only" (v. 36). He will come suddenly and unexpectedly—just as the Flood did—when people are going about their usual affairs, "eating and drinking, marrying and giving in marriage." There is a hint here that moral conditions may be comparable to those of Noah's day. But the point emphasized is the element of complete surprise (vv. 36–39). To illustrate, the Lord says that two men shall be in the field and two women grinding at the mill, and in each case "one will be taken and the other left" (vv. 40–41). That is, one will be taken away in judgment and the other left to go into the kingdom (see Matthew 13:41–43; 25:34–41).

3. **The Lord's admonition to watchfulness (vv. 42–44)**

Next, the Lord counsels watchfulness on the part of his own. Just as a thief depends on surprise in entering and robbing a house, so the Lord will come unexpectedly, catching Satan and his human followers off guard, and will break up his earthly kingdom, for Satan is the god of this world. See Matthew 12:26–28; 2 Corinthians 4:3–4. But believers have been forewarned and are to be on the alert.

4. **The faithful servant and the evil servant, at the return of Christ (vv. 45–51)**

The Lord Jesus contrasts good and bad servants, indicating that when he returns there will be faithful servants and also those who claim to be his servants but who actually are hypocrites, seeking only their own advantage. The first will be rewarded, but the latter exposed for what they are and punished.

THREE TESTS (25:1-46)

Chapter 25 records three tests, revealed by the Lord, that will be applied at the time of his Second Coming—the test of the virgins, the servants, and the nations.

1. The ten virgins (25:1-13)

The ten virgins apparently represent Israel. When Christ returns, Israel will profess to know God, worship him, and serve him. As the virgins go out to meet the Bridegroom, so Israel will be expecting her Messiah to come. But some will be looking for Jesus as their returning Messiah, or Christ, whereas the rest will be looking for a Messiah that is not the Lord Jesus. Oil is a symbol of the Holy Spirit. Thus, five virgins are instructed by the Holy Spirit to look for the return of Jesus; the other five, uninstructed, are, in a great measure at least, in spiritual darkness (vv. 1-4). When the midnight cry is made, all ten trim their lamps and prepare to meet the Bridegroom. The five who lack oil vainly look for some, but it is too late. Some in Israel will vainly look for the truth that only the Holy Spirit can reveal, but their opportunity will have passed. The Bridegroom comes, and those who are ready go in to the marriage with him—and then the door will be shut (vv. 5-10). The others come later and beg admittance, but it is too late. The day of grace for them is past, and the awful declaration of the Lord Jesus Christ, the heavenly Bridegroom, falls upon their startled ears: "I know you not."

How important to watch and be ready (vv. 11-13).

(Some Bible students interpret the parable of the wise and foolish virgins as representing the true and the false in professing Christendom during the church age, as in the parables of Matthew 13. There, they point out, it is the Bridegroom, not the Son of Man, for whom the virgins are waiting.)

2. The servants (25:14–30)

In the test of the servants, the man who travels to a far country is the Lord Jesus Christ; his servants are those who profess to know and worship and serve him, not as Israel does but as Christendom does. All of this, from 24:9 to 25:46, seems to have primary reference to the days between the Rapture of believers and the revelation of the Lord from heaven; yet principles are stated here that have undoubted application throughout our dispensation, or age of grace.

The five-talent man and the two-talent man are true servants, seeking to advance their master's interests. They are suitably rewarded, in two ways. Each receives the most comforting and rewarding of commendations: "Well done, you good and faithful servant . . . enter into the joy of your lord." See verses 21 and 23. In addition, each one is given a larger sphere of responsibility and service than before: "You have been faithful over a few things, I will make you ruler over many things." See verses 21 and 23 again.

The one-talent man remains. He is a false servant, a hypocrite, a pretender—not because he has but one talent, but perhaps just the reverse. That is, the Lord, knowing in advance that he is not a true servant, gives him only one talent, which is enough to reveal his hypocrisy. Note how the Lord condemns him: first, for being "wicked and slothful," in pretending to be a servant and yet not using the equipment given him to use in his service (vv. 24–27); second, for lacking what he should have had, and without which he could not be a true believer and servant. He had no faith, and without faith it is impossible to please God (see Hebrews 11:6); and he had no sense of duty to his master, so he could not serve God acceptably (see Luke 17:10). Hence, what he has, talent, is to be taken from him because he lacks the basic requirements that would make him first a believer and then a servant (vv. 28–29). Finally, this man receives the judgment appropriate to his hypocrisy (v. 30).

3. The Nations (25:31–46)

1. The nations in the presence of the Son of Man (vv. 31–33)

The third test is that of the nations, presumably with particular reference to the non-Christian nations. The Son of Man is to come in his glory, accompanied by all his holy angels. He is to sit on the throne of his glory, and all the nations are to be gathered before him. Whether this means representatives of all the nations will receive the King's judgment concerning the nations they represent, as national units, or whether it means all the individual persons of these nations, is an open question, although the more probable explanation seems to be that of individual persons. In any event, the King will separate them into two groups—sheep on the right, goats on the left (vv. 31–33).

"The sheep" (vv. 34–40)

The King deals with the sheep first. "Come, you blessed of my Father; inherit the kingdom prepared for you from the foundation of the world" (v. 34). Then he explains why he considers them his "sheep." They had been kind to him when he was in need (vv. 35–36). The Lord calls them "the righteous," indicating that these are justified people, and faith is the only means of justification. They ask when they had been kind to him, and he answers, "Inasmuch as you did it unto one of the least of my brothers, you did it unto me." That is to say, in receiving his brothers, the messengers of the "Gospel of the kingdom" (see Matthew 24:14)—his brothers according to the flesh who through faith in him have become his spiritual brothers (see Hebrews 2:11–12)—they have received him. His brothers have testified concerning him, as clearly indicated in Revelation 12:10–17. Thus the king receives his own, his sheep, into his kingdom (vv. 34–40).

3. "The goats" (vv. 41–45)

Turning to those on his left, the King speaks the saddest of all words: "Depart from me, you cursed, into everlasting fire, prepared for the devil and his angels" (v. 41). Immediately, he explains why they are "goats." When they saw him in need, they were indifferent and had not ministered to him (vv. 42–43). They ask him when they had seen him in need and had failed to minister to him, and he replies that, when they failed to minister to the least of his brothers, they failed to minister to him. Thus our Lord Jesus Christ intimately associates and identifies himself with his own (vv. 42–45).

4. Eternal destiny for both classes (v. 46)

The Lord makes one further comment: "These shall go away into everlasting punishment: but the righteous into life eternal." With these words of sharp division, and of eternal destiny for both classes, he brings his wonderful Olivet Discourse to a conclusion (v. 46).

13

The King Is Betrayed, Condemned, and Denied

26:1–75

THE KING'S DEATH IN VIEW (26:1–16)

1. **The King's prophecy of his death "after two days" (vv. 1–2)**

   The Lord has brought to an end his discussion of his Second Coming and now speaks to his disciples of his death, which is to occur almost at once. Several times before he has foretold his death. See Matthew 16:21; 17:22–23; 20:17–19. Now his betrayal is only two days away, and it will be followed by his crucifixion.

2. The Jewish leaders' conspiracy to kill Jesus (vv. 3–5)

About this time, the chief priests, the scribes, and the elders assemble at the palace, or court, of Caiaphas, the high priest. They conspire to arrest Jesus and put him to death, but they want to avoid two things: arresting him openly and putting him to death on the feast day—that is, the Passover Day. They fear "an uproar among the people."

3. Mary's discernment of his death, shown by her anointing him for burial (vv. 6–13)

About this time, while Jesus is in Bethany in the house of Simon the leper, a woman comes in and anoints his head with very precious ointment (vv. 6–7). The Lord's disciples are indignant at what they consider "this waste." They want to know why the ointment was not sold at a good price and the proceeds given to the poor (vv. 8–9). The Lord Jesus comes to the woman's defense, saying, she has done this in view of "my burial." She understood that he must die and be buried; and Jesus approves of her act as a "good work." Furthermore, he says that her deed will be told wherever the Gospel is preached throughout the world. This prophecy has been fulfilled, for the record of her act of discernment and love has found a place in the Bible itself (vv. 10–13).

4. Judas' bargain to betray the Lord (vv. 14-16)

Judas Iscariot does two things: He bargains with the chief priests for thirty pieces of silver to betray his Master, and then seeks a good opportunity to effect the betrayal.

In the first sixteen verses of this chapter, we have these four items, all of which foreshadow the Lord's death:
   a. *His own prophecy of it*
   b. *The religious leaders' plotting for it*
   c. *The woman's discernment of it*
   d. *Judas' bargain to betray him to it*

THE KING INSTITUTES THE LORD'S SUPPER (26:17-30)

1. The Last Passover and the Lord's Supper

We come now to the last proper celebration of the Passover, closing the old dispensation and terminating the covenant of the Law, and the first celebration of the Lord's Supper, opening the new dispensation of grace. These are only symbols, but they are full of significant meaning. The reality these symbols represent occurs the next day at Calvary.

2. The preparation of the Passover (vv. 17-20)

Jesus instructs his disciples—specifically Peter and John, according to Luke—to prepare the Passover at a certain house in the city. This they do; and at evening, or twilight, Jesus and his twelve disciples sit down to partake.

3. The Lord's prophecy of his betrayal by one of the Twelve (vv. 21-25)

As they are eating the Passover (see Exod. 12:1-11), Jesus tells them that one of them is going to betray him. They are extremely sad at this and begin, one by one to ask him, "Lord, is it I?" (vv. 21-22). The Lord gives them a sign to indicate which one it is and says that he is to go as prophesied in the Old Testament, "but woe unto that man by whom the Son of man is betrayed!" See Psalms 41:9 and 109:1-12. When Judas asks, "Master, is it I?" Jesus answers in the affirmative, "You have said it." The others asked, "Lord, is it I?" but Judas inquires, "Master [or Teacher], is it I?" (vv. 23-25).

4. The institution of the Lord's Supper (vv. 26-30)

As they continue eating the Passover, Jesus turns to the institution of the Lord's Supper. Taking bread, he blesses it—that is, he thanks God for it and asks his blessing on it—breaks it, and gives it to his disciples. As he does so, he says, "Take, eat; this is my body" (v. 26). That is to say, the loaf in the communion service, or the Lord's Supper, represents the body of the Lord Jesus Christ, in which he lived among men and women, and in which he bore our sins on the cross (see Hebrews 10:5; 1 Peter 2:24). As Jesus blessed the bread, he sanctified his body, setting it apart to do the will of God. As he broke it, so his body was to be broken—not the bones (John 19:32-36), but the flesh, torn by the thorns, the nails, and the spear. As he gave the bread to his disciples, he gave his body to be crucified for us. Thus, when we take the bread, it is in memory of him and of his sacrifice of himself for us (see 1 Corinthians 11:23-24).

After distributing the bread, he takes the cup, gives thanks for it, and gives it to his disciples, saying, "Drink all of it" (v. 27). He is not telling his disciples to drink the entire contents of the cup; rather he is telling them to partake of all of it. He explains why: "For this is my blood of the new testament [or covenant], which is shed for many for the remission of sins" (v. 28). The fruit of the vine (v. 29) in the cup, represents his blood, wrung violently from his body and shed in death to provide a just basis for God to forgive the sins of the many who trust Christ for their salvation. He will not drink of the fruit of the vine again until he drinks it, as he says, "new with you in my Father's kingdom." By this we understand that he refers to his Second Coming to set up the kingdom of heaven on earth.

After singing a hymn, perhaps a psalm of praise to God, they leave the house in the city of Jerusalem and go to the Mount of Olives (vv. 29–30).

THE KING PRAYS IN GETHSEMANE (26:31-46)

Matthew does not record all the events that took place or all the teaching Jesus gave on the night of his betrayal. John, in particular, gives us a number of additional items. Most of John 13–17 is devoted to such events and discourse, a large portion of which intervenes between the institution of the Lord's Supper and the events in Gethsemane.

1. **The conversation on the way to Gethsemane (vv. 31-35)**

Matthew records little of what transpired on the way to Gethsemane. He only mentions that Christ foretells how unfaithful the disciples would be that very night, in fulfillment of Old Testament Scripture (see Zechariah 13:7). Then he foretells his resurrection once more, and adds the fact that afterward he will precede them north into Galilee (vv. 31–32). Peter boasts that he will remain faithful, even though all the rest fail. Jesus replies with a mournful prophecy: before the cock crows the next morning, Peter will have denied him three times. Self-confident Peter, joined by all the rest, insists that he will not deny the Lord, even if faithfulness costs him his life (vv. 33–35).

2. The arrival in Gethsemane (vv. 36–38)

They arrive at Gethsemane, on the Mount of Olives, and Jesus says to his disciples: "Sit here while I go and pray." To Peter, James, and John, whom he takes with him, he says: "My soul is exceeding sorrowful, even unto death: wait here and watch with me."

3. The Lord's first prayer in Gethsemane (v. 39)

Going on alone, Jesus falls on his face and prays the most beautiful prayer ever uttered: "O my Father, if it be possible, let this cup pass from me: nevertheless not as I will, but as you will." Our Lord was perfectly human, as well as perfectly divine. He was God and at the same time man. Out of the sinlessness of his humanity, coupled with the holiness of his deity, he shrank from the cross—not because he dreaded the pain and ignominy, great as those would be, but because his holy being recoiled from the horrible experience of being made sin, or a sin-offering (see 2 Corinthians 5:21). Despite his anguish, he completely subjects his personal, human will to the will of his Father. So it should be with us.

4. His admonition to the sleeping disciples (vv. 40–41)

Returning to his disciples and finding them asleep, he rebukes Peter. Perhaps he addresses Peter particularly because he had boasted such a short time before about his devotion to the Lord Jesus. "What," says Jesus, "could you not watch with me one hour?" Then he continues with an admonition we too should heed: "Watch and pray, that you do not enter into temptation: the spirit indeed is willing, but the flesh is weak." We are not merely to be alert to keep from slipping into sin; nor are we simply to pray. We are to do both, realizing that while we may earnestly desire to do God's will, we are weak in the flesh and need divine help.

5. The second and third prayers and the Lord's rebuke of the still-sleeping disciples (vv. 42–46)

After this, our Lord prays twice again, offering substantially the same prayer each of the three times (vv. 42–44). Returning to his disciples after the third prayer, he speaks to them again about sleep. Perhaps it was really a question: "Are you still sleeping and taking your rest?" (v. 45 NASB). Continuing, he says, as if to rebuke them for thinking of sleep at such a time: "The hour is at hand, and the Son of man is betrayed into the hands of sinners. Rise, let us be going: behold, he is at hand who betrays me" (vv. 45–46).

THE KING BETRAYED AND ARRESTED (26:47–56)

While Jesus is speaking, Judas arrives with a large company of persons, sent by the chief priests and elders, and armed with swords and staves. With a kiss of identification, Judas betrays his Master to this rabble (vv. 47-49). They seize the Lord; whereupon one of his disciples—Peter, John tells us—draws his sword and cuts off an ear of the high priest's servant. The Lord rebukes Peter at this point, assuring him that through prayer he could, if he desired, obtain from his Father more than twelve legions of angels. "But," he says "how then shall the scriptures be fulfilled, that thus it must be?" (vv. 50-54). Luke tells us that Jesus touched the man's ear and healed him. Turning from Peter to the crowd, he upbraids them; whereupon all his disciples flee (vv. 55-56).

THE KING CONDEMNED BY THE JEWS (26:57-68)

1. The king on trial before Caiaphas (v. 57)

Jesus is taken to Caiaphas, the high priest, although John tells us he was first brought before Annas, who was the father-in-law of Caiaphas and evidently a man of great authority among the Jews. The scribes and elders and the entire Jewish council are assembled at the palace, or court, of the high priest.

2. Peter's following "afar off" (v. 58)

Peter follows "afar off" as Jesus is taken in. Peter, too, goes in and sits with the servants, to see the outcome.

3. The testimony of two false witnesses (vv. 59-61)

Seeking a witness to provide some pretext for putting Christ to death, they eventually find two who testify that he had said: "I am able to destroy the temple of God, and to build it in three days."

4. The king's claim to Messiahship and deity (vv. 62–64)

What he actually had said was: "Destroy this temple, and in three days I will raise it up" (John 2:19). John explains in verse 21 that "he spoke of the temple of his body." The Lord Jesus gives no answer to this accusation. When the high priest says, "I adjure you by the living God, that you tell us whether you are the Christ, the Son of God." Jesus replies, "You have said," meaning, "You have spoken the truth." Compare this with the answer he had given Judas in verse 25. To the high priest he adds: "Nevertheless I say to you, hereafter will you see the Son of man sitting on the right hand of power, and coming in the clouds of heaven." No other words could have given the high priest a more definite and affirmative answer to this question.

5. The definite rejection of the King by the Jewish nation (vv. 65–66)

Both Caiaphas and the members of the council understand perfectly his claim to be "the Christ, the Son of God," for they find him guilty of blasphemy and affirm that he is worthy of death. Thus the Jewish nation, through its high priest and council, rejects the King, brands him a blasphemer, and asserts that he ought to be put to death. In this the attitude described in John 10:31–39, Matthew 11:16–19, and elsewhere, is crystallized into definite action by the Jewish government.

6. Physical violence of the Jews—a manifestation of their hatred of the King (vv. 67-68)

The venom in the hearts of the members of this august council of Jewish leaders is clearly shown by their physical action at this point. They spit in his face; they buffet him; they smite him with the palms of their hands, saying in bitter mockery, "Prophesy unto us, you Christ, Who smote you?" In explaining this, Luke says they had blindfolded him.

THE KING DENIED BY PETER (26:69-75)

While these things were happening inside, other events were taking place outside in the court (NASB). A girl approaches Peter and says, "You also were with Jesus of Galilee." But Peter denies it before them all (vv. 69-70). Peter then goes out to the porch and, after being accused again of having been with Jesus, denies once more, this time with an oath, saying, "I do not know the man" (vv. 71-72). A little later he is again accused of being one of Jesus' group. They say to him, "Your speech betrays you." In other words, Peter's dialect or accent revealed him to be a Galilean. Peter begins to curse and swear, saying, "I know not the man." Immediately the cock crows and Peter remembers the words of Jesus, "Before the cock crow, you will deny me three times." See verses 34 and 35. Peter goes outside and weeps bitterly (vv. 73-75).

14

The King Dies and Rises Again

27:1-28:20

THE KING BEFORE PILATE (27:1-31)

1. The Jewish council's official condemnation of Jesus; their effort to obtain a Roman execution (vv. 1-2)

Everything done in connection with Jesus' Jewish trial, while it was still dark, evidently was unofficial (chap. 26); but at sunrise, official action is taken. "All the chief priests and elders of the people took counsel against Jesus to put him to death." Having found him guilty of blasphemy, they want the Romans to execute him, since the Jews had no authority to inflict the death penalty. Consequently, they bind Jesus and take him to Pontius Pilate, the Roman governor.

2. Judas' remorse and suicide (vv. 3-10)

Judas, seeing that Jesus has been condemned, repents of betraying him. He returns the thirty pieces of silver to the chief priests and elders and confesses that he sinned in betraying Jesus, an innocent person. They tell him they are not interested in him any longer, and Judas throws the money down in the Temple and goes out and hangs himself (vv. 3-5). Then the chief priests—willing to murder the Lord Jesus, yet so careful to observe the Law that they would not put the betrayal money into the treasury—use it to purchase a field in which to bury strangers. This fulfilled the Old Testament prophecy recorded in Jeremiah 32:6-9 (vv. 6-10).

3. Jesus' assertion of his Messiahship; his silence when falsely accused (vv. 11-14)

Pilate asks Jesus: "Are you the King of the Jews?" Jesus answers in the affirmative, just as he had answered the direct question of Caiaphas, the high priest, in Matthew 26:63-64. When accused by the chief priests and elders, however, Jesus is silent, even when urged by Pilate to answer. This fulfills Isaiah 53:7. When asked directly if he is "the Christ, the Son of God," or "the King of the Jews," he says he is; but when falsely accused, he says nothing. See 1 Peter 2:23.

4. The multitude's choice of Barabbas (vv. 15-21)

At Passover time, the Roman governor customarily released one prisoner to the Jews as a gesture of good will. The choice was theirs. Barabbas, a prominent insurrectionist and murderer (see Mark 15:7) was imprisoned by the Romans. Pilate offers to release to the Jews either "Barabbas, or Jesus which is called Christ." Pilate is in a difficult position. He knows the Jewish leaders are determined to see Jesus put to death, but his wife has warned him to have nothing to do with Jesus, "that just man." So he leaves the choice with the multitude. They, persuaded by the chief priests and elders, choose Barabbas. It is almost incredible that human beings should choose a character like Barabbas rather than the good and gracious Son of God, but such is the iniquity of the human heart!

5. Pilate's questions; the people's dire prophecy, unwittingly spoken (vv. 22-25)

Pilate then asks them what they want him to do with "Jesus which is called Christ." Their answer shows how thoroughly the Jewish leaders had done their evil work of influencing the crowd. "They all say unto him, Let him be crucified." When the governor asks for what crime, their insistence becomes more intense. In a futile gesture—washing his hands in water in front of them—Pilate seeks to excuse himself from all blame in connection with the death of Christ. To this the multitude responds with a statement that probably meant little to them at the time, but which has been fulfilled with startling accuracy throughout the following centuries: "His blood," said they, "be on us, and on our children."

6. Pilate's decision; the soldiers' cruel mockery of the King (vv. 26-31)

Pilate does three dreadful things. First, he releases Barabbas to the Jews; second, he has our Lord subjected to the terrible ordeal of a Roman scourging; third, he delivers him to be crucified (v. 26.) But before the actual crucifixion, Pilate's soldiers have some sport with their distinguished victim. That he was actually the son of God probably never occurred to them. They strip him and, in mockery, replace his own clothing with that of royalty. They plait a crown of thorns and put it on his head. They thrust a reed into his right hand. Then they mock him by bowing and saying, "Hail, King of the Jews!" Then, to show their contempt, they spit on him and strike him on the head with the reed they had mockingly put in his hand for a scepter. Following these indignities, they put his own clothing on him and take him out to be crucified (vv. 27–31).

THE KING IS CRUCIFIED (27:32-56)

1. The march to Calvary (vv. 32–34)

On the way to the place of crucifixion, a man of Cyrene, in North Africa, by the name of Simon, is compelled to carry the Lord's cross. They go outside the city wall, to a place called Golgotha, or Calvary (Luke 23:33), which means the "place of a skull." They offer him a drink consisting of a mixture of vinegar, or wine, and gall. The purpose was probably to deaden the pain of crucifixion. But Jesus, after tasting it, refused to drink. Rather, it seems, he would go to the cross with all his human faculties alert and vibrant, and drink to the bitter dregs the dreadful cup his Father was pressing to his lips, that he might thereby accomplish our redemption. See John 18:11.

2. The crucifixion (vv. 35–44)

Soldiers nail the Lord to the cross of a condemned criminal. Then they divide his clothing among them. When they come to his seamless robe, they gamble to see which one of the four of them shall have it all (see John 19:23–24). This fulfilled Psalm 22:18. Then they sit down and watch him (vv. 35–36).

Over his head they write the accusation: "THIS IS JESUS THE KING OF THE JEWS." In this way, Pilate expressed the charge he was using as a pretext for crucifying the Lord Jesus (John 19:19).

Jesus was not alone in crucifixion. Two thieves were crucified with him, one on either side. The heartless taunting begins. Those who pass by deride him, shaking their heads, suggesting that, if he is able to destroy the Temple and build it in three days, why does he not save himself? If he is really the Son of God, why does he not miraculously descend from the cross? The chief priests and elders join in the mockery, deriding his claims to be the King of Israel and the Son of God. Even the thieves, crucified with him, make common cause with the rest in mocking him (vv. 37–44).

None of them realized the glorious truth expressed hundreds of years later in a lovely hymn by A. Midlane:

Himself he could not save;
  He on the cross must die,
    Or mercy cannot come
      To ruined sinners nigh:
Yes, Christ, the Son of God, must bleed,
That sinners might from sin be freed.

Himself he could not save;
  Love's stream too deeply flow'd;
    In love himself he gave,
      To pay the debt we owed.
Obedience to his Father's will,
And love to him, did all fulfill.

A little later, one of the thieves apparently has a glimpse of this truth, for Luke tells us he rebuked the other thief and championed the Lord Jesus, asking him, "Remember me when you come into your kingdom" (Luke 23:39–43).

3. The three hours of darkness (vv. 45–50)

A three-hour period of darkness follows, as though God would hide his beloved Son from further ill-treatment and derision from callous unbelievers. Perhaps another reason for the darkness lies in God's unwillingness that there be any unfriendly witnesses of the awful yet sublime transaction about to take place as the prophecy of Isaiah 53:6 is fulfilled: "The LORD has laid on him the iniquity of us all."

At about the ninth hour, or about three in the afternoon, Jesus cries with a loud voice, "My God, my God, why have you forsaken me?" This is the only one of Christ's seven cries from the cross recorded by Matthew. Jesus does not say, "My Father, My Father" because the Father did not ever break fellowship with his beloved Son. Rather, the righteous God, the Ruler of the universe, turned away his face as the Lord Jesus became our sin-offering, and was thus identified with his people's sin. See Psalm 22:1–3; 2 Corinthians 5:21.

The people who hear this cry have various reactions. Some misunderstand, thinking he is calling for Elias, or Elijah, to come to save him. One runs for a sponge, fills it with vinegar, and places it on a reed, offering him some to drink. The rest say, "Let be, let us see whether Elijah will come to save him."

Jesus cries again, this time dismissing his spirit. Perhaps this is Matthew's way of summing up the last two cries in which our Lord says: "It is finished" (John 19:30); and "Father, into your hands I commend my spirit" (Luke 23:46). Thus he yields his spirit to God.

4. The rending of the veil of the Temple and other supernatural phenomena (vv. 51–53)

"And, behold, the veil of the temple was rent in two from the top to the bottom." The veil in the Tabernacle, and later the veil in the Temple, has symbolized, ever since the days of Moses, the barrier that stands between a holy God and a guilty sinner. Now that Christ has died, "the just for the unjust, that he might bring us to God" (1 Peter 3:18), the barrier is removed—torn apart by the hand of God himself—making it possible for us to go into the very presence of God "by a new and living way, which he has consecrated for us, through the veil, that is to say, his flesh" (see Hebrews 10:20).

When Christ died on the cross, his blood was "shed for many for the remission of sins" (Matthew 26:28), and the old dispensation of Law came to an end. No longer would there be any need to shed the blood of bulls and goats in place of the one real sacrifice for sins. That sacrifice, which reconciles the believing sinner to God, has now been made, and a new day dawns. A new dispensation of marvelous grace has been ushered in. The earth quakes; rocks shake; graves open; and, after Christ's resurrection, many saints arise from the dead and appear to people in Jerusalem.

5. The testimony of the centurion and his soldiers to the deity of Jesus (v. 54)

The Roman centurion, the officer in charge of the soldiers who had nailed the Lord to the cross, as well as the soldiers with him, see these things and are terrified. "Truly," they say, "this was the Son of God." They, at least, are at last convinced that his claims were true.

6. The presence of the women "afar off" (vv. 55–56)

At a distance, many of the women who had followed the Lord from Galilee are watching, including Mary Magdalene, Mary the mother of James and Joses, and the mother of James and John, the sons of Zebedee.

THE KING IS BURIED (27:57–66)

1. The burial of the King (vv. 57–61)

At evening, Joseph of Arimathea, a man of wealth and a secret disciple of the Lord (see John 19:38), begs Pilate for the body of Jesus. Joseph evidently was a member of the Jewish council, which had condemned the Lord, although he had not voted with the majority (see Luke 23:50–51). This was Friday evening, the day before the Sabbath, or Saturday (see Mark 15:42). Joseph takes the Lord's body, wraps it in a clean linen cloth, and lays it in his new rock-hewn tomb. Rolling a large stone against the mouth of the sepulcher, he goes his way, leaving Mary Magdalene and the other Mary (see v. 56) seated nearby.

2. The Roman guard at the tomb (vv. 62–66)

The next day, the Sabbath, the chief priests and Pharisees go to Pilate. Referring to Jesus as a deceiver, they remind Pilate of something Jesus had prophesied before his death: "After three days I will rise again." They request Pilate to make sure the Lord's disciples do not come by night, steal away his body, and then say to the people, "He is risen from the dead." If that were to happen, they say, "The last error shall be worse than the first" (vv. 62–64). It would be worse for them to have the report of Jesus' resurrection circulating than it was to have him claim, before his crucifixion, to be "the Christ, the Son of God." And so it proved to be; for when Peter publicly proclaimed at Pentecost the fact of Jesus' resurrection by the power of God, three thousand persons were saved and became followers of the Lord Jesus (see Acts 2:32–41).

Pilate replies, "You have a watch" (guard, NASB). According to Matthew 28:12, Pilate provided them with a detail of Roman soldiers to guard the tomb. So these chief priests and Pharisees go to the sepulcher with the soldiers, who seal the stone and stand guard at the tomb (vv. 65–66).

The huge stone used to close Eastern tombs of this sort is rolled downhill in a groove in the earth cut for that purpose. The seal of the Roman soldiers is a mark of some sort on the stone to indicate that the power of the Roman government is pledged to keep that tomb closed. To break or violate that seal probably meant death for anyone found guilty.

Roman soldiers keep vigil at the tomb to make sure no one interferes and that the dead body of the Lord Jesus Christ remains inside. How futile all these precautions proved to be, as we see in chapter 28.

THE KING IS RISEN (28:1-15)

1. The angel's message to the women concerning the resurrection of the King (vv. 1–7)

Just before dawn Sunday morning, Mary Magdalene and the other Mary (see Matthew 27:61) return to the sepulcher. A great earthquake occurs, and the angel of the Lord comes down from heaven, rolls the stone back up from the entrance to the tomb, and sits on it. Bright as lightning in appearance and clad in snow-white garments, he strikes terror into the hearts of the soldiers on guard. They tremble and become as helpless as dead men. Then the angel says to the women: "Fear not: for I know you seek Jesus, which was crucified. He is not here: for he is risen, as he said." Having said this, and having thus declared the greatest news ever to fall on human ears, he invites them to come and see. Then he directs them to go and tell. The women are to tell Jesus' disciples the news of the Lord's resurrection and to tell them he will precede them to Galilee where they will see him.

2. The risen Lord's appearance to the women (vv. 8–10)

The women leave the sepulcher—fearfully, for they have seen an angel of God who has given them a very important duty to perform. Yet they are filled with great joy, for their news contains a message of unbounded gladness and hope. They run to take the news to the disciples, but on the way Jesus himself meets them, saying, "All hail." They approach him, hold him by the feet—which seems to indicate that they fall prostrate before him—and worship him (vv. 8–9).

The Lord Jesus speaks comfortingly to them, saying, "Be not afraid: go tell my brethren that they go into Galilee, and there shall they see me." Thus he confirms his own words, spoken just before he prayed in Gethsemane (see Matthew 26:32), and the angel's words to the women (see Matthew 28:7). The disciples are to see him in Galilee (v. 10).

3. The Jewish leaders' invention of a false report concerning the body of Jesus (vv. 11-15)

As the women go on their way to deliver their glorious good news to the Lord's disciples, some guards at the sepulcher make their way into Jerusalem and report to the chief priests all that had happened.

The chief priests consult with the elders and then give a large bribe to the soldiers with these instructions: "Say that his disciples came by night, and stole him away while we slept."

This was a ridiculous story, of course; but since they steadfastly refused to believe the truth, it was probably the best tale they could devise to try to explain the disappearance of the Lord's body.

It was ridiculous for at least two reasons. First, if they were asleep, how could they know what had happened? Second, for Roman soldiers to fall asleep while on guard meant immediate execution.

Other reasons making this story incredible are: (1) the improbability that all the soldiers should be asleep at one time and that none would awaken in all the commotion the disciples would have to create to move the stone and remove the body; (2) the improbability that the disciples, frightened and scattered, would even attempt such a bold and dangerous undertaking (vv. 11–13).

The chief priests and elders try to reassure the soldiers with these added words: "If this come to the governor's ears, we will persuade him, and secure you."

In other words, if Pilate should hear about the disappearance of Jesus' body from the tomb, they would bribe him to overlook it, as they were now bribing the soldiers, and would protect them from the possible consequences.

The soldiers accept the bribe and circulate the story concocted by the chief priests and elders.

When Matthew wrote his Gospel some years later, the fiction of the chief priests and elders still was a common story among the unbelieving Jews (vv. 14–15).

THE KING COMMISSIONS HIS DISCIPLES (28:16–20)

1. The risen Lord's appearance to the eleven in Galilee (vv. 16–17)

Evidently the women faithfully performed their duty and gave the eleven disciples the message of the Lord Jesus and of the angel, for they proceed to Galilee, to "a mountain where Jesus had appointed them."

There he appears to them; and when they see him, they worship him.

Some doubt, however. One who doubted his resurrection, though probably not on this occasion, was Thomas. See John 20:24–29.

The reluctance of some of the Lord's disciples to believe he had actually risen from death increases the weight and strengthens the value of their testimony when the evidence becomes so overpowering that they are, as it were, compelled to believe it.

2. His Great Commission (vv. 18–20a)

Jesus gives to the eleven his commission for world-wide evangelism and instruction.

Mark, Luke, and John, as well as Paul (see 1 Corinthians 15:5–8), tell us of other resurrection appearances of the Lord to various individuals and groups of his disciples, but Matthew tells us only of his appearances to the women and to the eleven disciples.

To the latter he says, "All power is given unto me in heaven and in earth. Go therefore, and teach all nations, baptizing them in the name of the Father, and of the Son, and of the Holy Spirit: teaching them to observe all things I have commanded you: and lo, I am with you always, even unto the end of the world. Amen."

a. In the New American Standard Bible "power" is "authority."

"All authority has been given to me in heaven and on earth." Hence, he instructs them to do certain things, backed by his complete heavenly and earthly authority.

b. *He tells them to go.*

They are not to wait for others to seek them out—they are to go to others.

c. *They are to teach, or make disciples of, all nations.*

They are to make learners of all the nations, Gentiles as well as Jews, that all people might learn the sublime truths regarding the righteousness and grace of God, the facts concerning the birth, life, teachings, death, and resurrection of Christ, and the terms of God's salvation through faith in a crucified and risen Savior.

d. *They are to baptize those who receive their message in, or into, the name of the Triune God—Father, Son, and Holy Spirit.*

This symbolic act is a public announcement that they recognize their transfer of allegiance from Satan—or false gods, self-effort, the world, or anything and everything else—to the true God who is Father, Son, and Holy Spirit.

e. *They are to teach believers to observe all the commandments Jesus gave them.*

These include the celebration of the Lord's Supper (Matthew 26:26–28), the law of love among believers (John 15:12–17), and many others.

3. The assurance of his presence always (v. 20b)

Having instructed his disciples, Jesus now assures them of his presence with them, conditioned, it would seem, on their obedience. "Lo, I am with you always," or all the days. They, and we, may confidently count on his presence day by day, if and when we are faithfully carrying out his commission.

As someone once observed: "No go, no lo!"

One point remains. Jesus says he will be with them, and with us, "unto the end of the world," or, more correctly, to the end or consummation of the age. It is more a time element than a space element, it would seem. Throughout this age, he will be with his own who faithfully serve him, until he comes again for them at the consummation of this age of grace. See 1 Thessalonians 4:16–17.

4. No record of the King's ascension in Matthew

This is the end of the story as far as Matthew is concerned. Mark and Luke relate his ascension, but not Matthew. Perhaps this is to emphasize the point that we are not to be occupied only with the thought that our Savior is now in heaven, crowned with glory and honor—although that, of course, is gloriously true—but rather with the thought that he has given us a task to perform, and that he is present with us to give us all the help we need to perform it—until the day Jesus returns to establish his Kingdom in power and glory. May that glad day soon dawn!